This Book is Geraldine

1-8-19

Also by Charlamagne Tha God

Black Privilege

SHOOK ONE

ANXIETY PLAYING TRICKS ON ME

CHARLAMAGNE THA GOD

TOUCHSTONE

New York London Toronto Sydney New Delhi

Touchstone
An Imprint of Simon & Schuster, Inc.
1230 Avenue of the Americas
New York, NY 10020

First Touchstone hardcover edition October 2018

TOUCHSTONE and colophon are registered trademarks of Simon & Schuster, Inc.

For information about special discounts for bulk purchases,
please contact Simon & Schuster Special Sales at 1-866-506-1949
or business@simonandschuster.com.

The Simon & Schuster Speakers Bureau can bring authors to your live event.
For more information or to book an event, contact the Simon & Schuster Speakers Bureau
at 1-866-248-3049 or visit our website at www.simonspeakers.com.

Manufactured in the United States of America

1   3   5   7   9   10   8   6   4   2

Library of Congress Cataloging-in-Publication Data has been applied for.

ISBN 978-1-5011-9325-5
ISBN 978-1-5011-9327-9 (ebook)

This book is dedicated to those who live by faith, not by fear.

CONTENTS

Foreword by Brad "Scarface" Jordan   xi

Introduction: My Anxiety Is Playing Tricks on Me   xvii

CHAPTER 1
Shook   1

CHAPTER 2
So Anxioussssssss (Ginuwine Voice)   9

CHAPTER 3
Blackanoid   57

CHAPTER 4
The Fear of Therapy   99

CHAPTER 5
Losing My Roots   135

CHAPTER 6
Parental Paranoia   183

CHAPTER 7
Fear of Failure   229

Acknowledgments   255

FOREWORD

I sat down with the legendary rapper Scarface to talk to him about the Geto Boys' song "Mind Playing Tricks on Me" and how, for me and a lot of people in the hood, it was one of the first songs that articulated the anxiety and paranoia that a lot of us were feeling.

"Mind Playing Tricks on Me" was due to be on my solo album. I wrote three verses to that song first and recorded it. It was my first verse, my second verse, and this is the third verse that made the song. I put my paranoia and anxiety in my music, man. It wasn't shit to talk about. I didn't feel like it was a problem. I just felt like it was normal to feel like this. It was normal to look at every person you've come in contact with as a potential for some material.

I was making music that addressed how I felt. Like, this is me, this is what I was going through, and this is what I wrote my music based on. What I was going through and how I was feeling. I wrote my heart and that's what came from it.

It's easy to put out a song talking about struggle and vulnerability when you went through it. Like the easiest songs to write are the songs you've been through, the situations that you've been through. The music is about me, and there is a long list of fucking paranoia, schizophrenia in my family. I've got an uncle right now that's really going through it, man. He ain't been the same since the late seventies. I can put it on a lot of shit, man. But I think that the more drugs you do, the more that shit triggers.

It's in the chemistry. That's how my grandma was. She was the oldest child, and she and her sister outlived all of their other siblings. So the way I dealt with mental—I can't even call it mental health issues. I just call it the reality of the life shit. The way that I dealt with it, man, was to accept the things that I could change and be smart enough to know the shit that I couldn't.

For me, I can't go to a doctor and have this doctor telling me how to feel. I can't go to a psychiatrist to tell me how I'm supposed to feel, if I don't feel like that. For me, it just doesn't work to be coached on how to feel, because feel is a feel. You can coach me on all kinds of shit, but you can't coach me how to feel.

I did do therapy when I was in the hospital for this shit. I think I did about twenty months in a hospital. At a psych ward. And that right there let me know that nobody can make me feel how I don't. And nobody can make me feel how I do, you feel me?

I don't think the therapy helped me. It did make me realize that I wasn't crazy. Therapy made me realize how normal I was. Therapy made me realize that it is what it is. You know, be smart enough to accept the things that you cannot change. You know what fixes everything?

Money. Money makes it easy. All that shit that you was worried about, that shit's gone with me now. You know what to do with money, don't you? You put people around you that you want around you. When you got money you can get the fuck out the way.

I mean, this is what I know, man. That shit on your report card: "Works or plays well with others"? I don't work and play well with others. I don't. I need to be around my people, man, in my element. I can't function no other kind of way.

Yeah, I'm here man. I know how to survive in this shit. You know what I'm saying? But I'm not worried—I'm going to have money, I'm not going to jump. I'll just go get another bag.

I think we all going to deal with anxiety. I deal with anxiety every time I put my mask on for the CPAP machine. I deal with anxiety when I'm in the back of a fucking airplane. You know what I'm saying? That's anxiety. When you know for a fact that you can't sit up against this fucking window. That's anxiety. You know, you can't move, man. I need to wait to go out to the plane until right before they close the door and start rolling. And I have to look out a fucking window. That's anxiety, all right? I cannot sit in the back, man. How many rows in the plane? How many rows? Not the big plane with first class. I am talking about the little commuter plane.

If you know there's something that makes you fucked up about certain things, don't put yourself in that position. Don't put yourself in that predicament, homie. Like if you know fucking well that you can't drive for a long period of time without feeling, you know, homesick after being away for a few, you know what I mean? Don't do it.

You got to adjust, man. You don't put yourself in that position. I'm not going to the back of that fucking plane. I'm going to wait until they have a seat in the front, that way I can be next to the door.

I think that people in the hood experience post-traumatic stress disorder. I think that the people in the hood, they are experiencing years and years of fucking despair. That's the PTSD, or whatever the fuck that is. The post-traumatic stress in the neighborhood, just being in the same conditions and expect the shit to change every day. You know, you're waking up and you just—you wake up today and the same shit was going on in 1970. Ain't nothing changed.

If I made a new version of "Mind Playing Tricks on Me" now it would be bigger than me. You know. The paranoia, my paranoia would be based on my people going back into slavery. You know, my paranoia would be based on one of my children being pulled over by the police and shot down. You know, my paranoia would be one of my daughters being disrespected and shot up in her fucking school. That's my paranoia now. You know it's bigger than me now. I don't give a fuck about me right now. I give a fuck about what's behind me. You know, that's where I'm on the ground fighting. So that shit don't happen to mine or yours, to us, to ours. And I'm going to fight.

I'm going to fight, homie. I'm not going to let nobody fuck over your daughter, my nigga. I'm coming. Don't do it. I've already made it up in my mind, and I'm down to lay my life down for my people. Don't fuck with us. We are not afraid of the white man. We afraid of the white-man law, of the white-man rule.

We need to figure out a way to petition to get all these white-boy cops out of the black neighborhoods, and I'm going to leave it like that. No. I don't want to make it sound like that, but all

the fucking claims with police officers in these black neighborhoods, shooting these black boys down, I want them gone—

Again, I'm just being real. Those are the issues that are creating the most anxiety in my life.

I feel like when I put my anxiety out there it opens up the
lines of communication to the people that feel the same way. It
opens it up. It opens up the conversation. So I'm scared of that
shit. You know, that's what I'm fearful of. And I'm asking everyone else, are you fearful of the same things?

—Brad "Scarface" Jordan

INTRODUCTION

My Anxiety Is Playing Tricks on Me

If you're not familiar with the Geto Boys' undisputed classic "Mind Playing Tricks on Me" (and shame on you if you're not) the song is all about anxiety and paranoia. Scarface, Bushwick Bill, and Willie D lay out the exact fears that I, and others like me, have experienced. It starts with Scarface's bars, "At night I can't sleep / I toss 'n' turn." Bruh, stress and anxiety definitely cause sleep problems. I'm a living testament to that. Then 'Face continues, "I'm paranoid sleeping with my finger on the trigger / My mother's always stressing I ain't living right / But I ain't going out without a fight." That line could have been about my father. He definitely wasn't living right for many years and used to sleep with a Buck knife under his pillow. He was convinced Satan was going to visit him in his sleep and didn't want to get taken out without a fight.

Later Scarface talks about a mysterious person trying to kill him, even visiting him in his sleep. "I'm deep in the covers / When I awake I don't see the muthafucker." Man, I've been there. For years I had dreams of someone pulling up alongside me and shooting up my car. I can still see the guy's face: Corn-rows, a thin mustache, and no facial hair, framed by a black hoodie. I know other people had similar experiences. My boy

Jerrell used to tell me he would also see someone trying to kill him in his sleep and vowed to get him first. He would say he knew *exactly* what the guy looked like. Jerrell ended up being shot and killed in 2015. His murderer is still at large, so I often wonder if it was, in fact, the same person from his dreams.

Scarface said he might need to "take a chill B." When we were kids, we would always say that: *Man, you need to take a chill pill!* We didn't realize those were real, but they were: and they were called *meds!* My grandma used to be on them, except her generation called them "nerve pills." I'm sure they were Valium or some other drug that didn't really solve the problem, more likely just got her addicted. Thank God I've never tried to rely on those!

I could also definitely relate when he rhymed, "Every twenty seconds got me peepin' out my window / investigating the joint for traps / checkin' my telephone for taps." Damn, so many of us who sold crack in the late 1990s and early 2000s knew that talking street business on the phone was a no-no. We were always paranoid someone was listening in!

It was no different with Willie D's verse. He thought he was getting followed because of his status. "I take my boys everywhere I go / because I'm paranoid." That is me right now! You're rarely going to see me without my friend Wax by my side to make sure someone isn't going to run up on me. I was never a "trap star" but I am a radio star, and I've already been run up on twice. I'm not trying to make it three times.

Willie D also says he's convinced that he's being followed by killers when he's driving. Well, me too. Just the other day I was telling my therapist about a panic attack I had after leaving the Walgreens in the town where I live in New Jersey. As I tell this story, keep in mind I pay about $17K a year in property taxes. So when I say it's a nice area, it's nice. There's nobody slangin' or trappin'. The scariest thing you will encounter are deer jumping out in front of your car at night.

On this particular evening, I was getting home late, which for me was about nine thirty at night. After pulling out of the Walgreens, I stopped at a light and looked down at my phone. All of a sudden I hear a massive bass thump coming from the car behind me. I looked in my rearview mirror and saw this car was right up on my bumper. Had some people followed me from the Walgreens? Were they about to run up on me? Was this it? As Willie D said in his verse, "Ain't no use to me lying / I was scareder than a muthafucker!"

I looked through both of my side mirrors to make sure no one had hopped out and was creeping up on the side of me with a pistol. I was imagining a scene like when Caine creeped up on that dude at the drive-through window in *Menace II Society*. I didn't see anyone, and when the light finally turned green, I shot off. But the car stayed behind me. It drove behind me for a few minutes, the bass throbbing the entire time. As I approached another red light, the road widened to two lanes. The driver stayed behind me until the last moment and then veered off to the left and pulled up alongside me. I gripped my wheel, expecting shots to ring out at any second.

Willie D finishes his verse by saying that when he finally pulled over to confront the person following, what he saw would "make your ass start giggling / Three blind, crippled, and crazy senior citizens." In my case, it wasn't senior citizens, but what I saw was just as ridiculous.

When the gunshots never came, I finally turned to get a look at my tormentor. Sitting in the car across from me was a white boy with glasses. I'm talking Paul Pfeiffer from *The Wonder Years*-type of white boy with glasses. Or Milhouse from *The*

Simpsons. Maybe a threat if he got a high-powered assault rifle and some ammo and decided to shoot up a school, but not even remotely a threat to me on that evening. I let out a huge sigh of relief and headed home. Nothing more than another case of me being paranoid for no reason.

When I told that story to my therapist, you know what she said? That she grew up in that town and that I needed to relax. To, as Scarface said, "take a chill B." Because no matter what I thought, there was never a chance anyone was going to pull up on me in a town like that. It was all in my head.

The song's final verse belongs to Bushwick Bill. This dude's anxiety was so bad that he thought it was Halloween when it wasn't! He rhymed about going out trick-or-treating, only to be tormented by what sounds like some sort of apparition. "He stood about six or seven feet," rhymed Bill. "Now that's the nigga I be seein' in my sleep."

Those lines remind me of the boogeymen my parents would tell me to watch out for when I was a little kid. I always would think there were people hiding in our closets and under my bed. Were my parents unwittingly responsible for some of my later anxiety? It could be, which is why I don't talk to my kids about ghosts in the attic or boogeymen hiding in the closets. I don't want to plant seeds of fear in their heads. There are other ways to get their attention and have them follow rules.

Bill's verse ends with his hallucinating that he's jumping this guy, though he eventually realizes that he was just punching the sidewalk and beating his own hands into bloody pulps. Might sound extreme, but I've been in a similar situation.

It was my birthday and I had just finished my 6:00 to 10:00 p.m. shift at Hot 103.9 in Columbia, South Carolina. I decided to go over to my homeboys Wax and Dre's house to catch up with them. I wasn't really smoking weed at the time, but since it was my birthday, Wax and Dre convinced me to smoke an L with them.

Big mistake. After we finished the blunt, they left the room for whatever reason. As I sat there by myself, I started panicking. That weed had taken my normal level of anxiety and turned it all the way up. They had been gone for only a few minutes, but it seemed like an eternity.

I became convinced something was seriously wrong, so without telling anyone, I jumped up and ran out of the house like it was on fire. I hopped into my little silver Honda Accord and started driving down I-77, toward my apartment. I was trying to stay calm, but the lights of the other cars on the road seemed to make my anxiety kick in even crazier. I became convinced that I had made a major mistake by trying to celebrate my birthday, which is a no-no for Jehovah's Witnesses. I was sure I was going to get pulled over, and when the cop realized I was high, be thrown in jail.

My heart was beating fast, my palms were sweaty, and I felt like I was speeding down the road, out of control. Just then I looked over to my passenger seat, and who did I see sitting there but a vision of myself! My double looked exactly how I looked, except it had a black hoodie on. My double looked back at me and in a chopped-and-screwed voice said, "SLOOOOOOOOOOOW-WWWWWW DOOOOOOOWWWWWWWWWNNNNNN."

I checked the speedometer, but I was only doing forty miles per hour, so I told my double, "You tripping! I'm only doing forty. I need to go faster so I can get home!"

"No, slow down," replied my double. "You're gonna get pulled over."

"I am slowed down, shut the fuck up!" I yelled back. Then, just to show my double who was in charge, I sped up to about fifty-five. My double just kept shaking his head at me, but I (we?) eventually made it home safe and sound. As soon as I pulled into my driveway, I hopped out of my car to deal with my double once and for all. I pulled open the passenger door and punched him hard in the face three or four times. Then I snapped out of it and realized I had been beating the shit out of my headrest. To paraphrase the Geto Boys, "God damn, homey, my anxiety playing tricks on me!"

Anxiety and paranoia have plagued me throughout my whole life, but now I'm trying to figure out what's real and what's just my mind playing tricks on me.

SHOOK
ONE

CHAPTER 1

Shook

"I am not at peace. I simply am a damaged human swimming in a pool of emotions every day of my life. There's a ragin violent storm inside of my heart at all times. Idk what peace feels like. Idk how to relax. My anxiety and depression have ruled my life for as long as I can remember."

—Kid Cudi

"Damn, I'm about to OD on weed, and my wife hates me for not making her squirt."

That's all I could think about lying in my bed at the SLS, my favorite hotel in Los Angeles.

Now before you jump to conclusions, I'm not one of these new niggas that partakes in every type of drug under the sun. Nope, I've never sniffed coke. (I did smoke it once in a blunt by accident. Best high of my life, don't let anybody tell you otherwise. If I wasn't officially an oldhead, I would do it again by accident.) Just like I've never sipped lean or popped a Perc. (Except for the one time when I was in a car accident and had them legitimately. I was literally having sex all day. That right there is a key factor as to why so many dudes use them.) Nope, hard drugs just aren't my thing. My tastes run more to cognac and weed.

All I'd done that night was sit with my wife on our hotel room's back patio and smoke a joint. It had some nut-ass name like Blue Dream, White Widow, or Green Crack. Granted, I haven't smoked much since being put on probation for a fire-arm charge back in high school. But one joint, even if it was LA chronic (whoever named it the City of Angels has never smoked a high grade of sativa because that shit ain't nothing but the devil), shouldn't have had me curled up in the fetal position like Smokey in the chicken coop in *Friday*.

But that's *exactly* where I found myself.

Before I go any further, let me explain why I was in LA in the first place. I was promoting my debut book, *Black Privilege*, which had been on the *New York Times* bestseller list for close to a month. I'd spent the previous weeks traveling around the country appearing before absolutely insane crowds at book-stores. Seven hundred people in Houston. Five hundred in Charlotte. Another five hundred at one bookstore in Atlanta, then another four hundred at another bookstore a few miles away the same day.

I don't know about you, but I'm not used to seeing that many Negroes in a bookstore. People were lined up to buy my book the way black folks usually line up to buy Jordans or Yeezys. I should have been the happiest man in the world, right?

Just the opposite.

I wasn't happy. OK, let me rephrase that: I was happy, but with a side of worry. With that worry came appetizers called nervousness. Oh, and for dessert they brought out some unease. Yes, for years I'd dreamed about becoming a bestselling author.

I'd grown up loving books and had always wanted to see my own words inspiring and motivating people. But now that I'd achieved that goal, I was finding that being a successful author is served with a full course of ANXIETY.

This sort of anxiety attack always happens whenever I reach a new level of success. I start overthinking about the new devils that come with the new levels. Great things can be happening all around me and my mind gets stuck playing a loop of the worst-possible scenarios.

So it was no surprise that by the time I got to LA, I'd become obsessed with the idea that the tour was going to fall apart. Just because six hundred people showed up to hear me speak in Washington, DC, didn't mean six hundred people would show in LA. Or even if they did, maybe it would be on the day that the Big One, that apocalyptic earthquake we've been hearing about all these years, would finally happen. "What do I do during an earthquake?" I was spiraling. "Am I supposed to stand in the middle of the doorway? Do I stop, drop, and roll? Or is it "stop, drop, shut 'em down, open up shop"? Should I yell out 'That's how Ruff Ryders roll'?"

If the Big One didn't get me, then I even convinced myself that a white supremacist was going to decide they want to make a political statement and let the mayonnaise fly by shooting up the *Black Privilege* book tour stop in Burbank.

LOOK, I DON'T KNOW WHY MY BRAIN WORKS THIS WAY, BUT IT DOES.

When I shared my stresses with some of my LA friends, they assured me that weed would lessen my anxiety. Now, what they failed to tell me is that weed isn't like what I was smoking back in the day in Moncks Corner, South Carolina. Back home, I only knew of two types: good weed and wack weed. One got you high, and the other didn't. Nowadays it's all types of flavors and grades, uppers and downers, sativa and indica. Indica is the one that is supposed to make you relax, and is probably what I should have been smoking. Unfortunately, I didn't know that until after the fact. In the moment, I chose the other strain.

It wasn't a problem until my wife and I started fooling around. I've been with my woman since 1998, and we've been married for four of those twenty years, and I definitely still care about things like making her orgasm. But never in our time together do I remember us having sex with high-grade weed in our systems.

At first everything was cool, but then I decided to go down on her. I swear I was doing a decent job, but after what felt like an eternity, my weed-triggered brain went from "Damn she's taking a long time to cum," to "Oh, shit, I can't make my woman cum anymore! My tongue is broke!" Never mind the fact she's been squirting in my face for the last eighteen years and I've been taking it like a champ.

In that moment though, all my prior good work seemed to be lost. What purpose would I serve my woman sexually if I couldn't make her cum? My jaw and neck were starting to hurt, but thankfully she changed the energy of the room and had me stop so she could return the favor. I'd say I only lasted twenty-seven seconds tops until I busted off.

Now, my wife knows me; I'm "one and done," especially now that I'm in the 40/40 Club (all that "nut and then get hard again" shit is out the window).

My wife didn't trip, all she said was, "You owe me." But the weed and anxiety translated that to "We are getting a divorce because you can no longer please me sexually. IT'S OVER, NIGGA" in my mind.

That's how I ended up on my back, looking like a cockroach trying to scramble onto its feet, legs all flying in the air. I was Milly Rocking between twelve-hundred-thread-count sheets. When I say Milly Rocking, what I really mean is shaking uncontrollably like Rocky at the beginning of *Rocky V* when he was sitting in the locker room after fighting the Russian. Like Muhammad Ali holding the torch at the 1996 Olympics in Atlanta.

Seeing me Harlem Shake against my will, my wife started laughing. It was only because she was high, but my paranoid mind raced to the million-dollar life-insurance policy we'd just taken out. She was trying to kill me to collect the money! That made my heart start beating like crazy. "I'm going to die of a heart attack!" my mind screamed. "I'm nowhere near famous enough to OD in a LA hotel room!" Every time I would almost fall asleep, I would see black shadowy hands trying to pull me somewhere, causing me to literally jump out of the bed and scream. At one point my wife said to me, "You aren't going to run out of here naked, are you?" I considered it, then I thought of Martin Lawrence talking about running down the streets of LA naked and high as hell in his stand-up special *Runteldat*. The last thing I needed was that on my résumé, so I put my clothes on just in case and laid back down to sleep. My heart was beating so loud, so hard, and so fast that I just knew a heart attack was inevitable. I started counting down from ten, and it felt like when I struck one my heart was going to explode and I was going to die of a sativa overdose. Not to mention a broken heart courtesy of my broken tongue causing my wife not to orgasm.

Of course it didn't happen. I eventually fell asleep and then woke up at 2:00 a.m. LA time with my heart still intact to go tape my syndicated radio show *The Breakfast Club* for the East Coast. I did the book signing later that day, and it ended up being a success, without a member of Vanilla Isis in sight. That's what anxiety does: scares the living shit out of us for absolutely no reason at all.

But even though I went on with my tour and the rest of my life, that LA freak-out really stuck with me. It made me begin to think: Just how much does anxiety affect us? I've literally felt anxious every day for as long as I can remember. How have I been functioning like that? Is it a poison that paralyzed me? Or a fuel that propels me to greatness?

Until recently I've always believed that my accomplishments have come from being fearless. Yet as I get older, and a little more self-conscious, I've come to believe that I've actually gotten here because I was *scared*. The fear of ending up under a tree in Moncks Corner doing nothing, or back on the street, or of things not working out in radio and on TV has pushed me to succeed. But what I've also realized is that while fear has been a good motivator and it can be a good motivator for you, it doesn't work forever. Anxiety had become too much for me to handle, and I knew if I wanted to keep going and keep growing I needed to deal with my shit. Fear had gotten me here, but it wasn't going to get me any further. That's why I started therapy.

And the more I opened up to people about my anxieties, it very quickly became evident that I am far from alone. From rappers to radio hosts to running backs to runway models, so many successful people I know admitted to me that they are filled with angst too.

Most of them are fellow hip-hop heads, part of a culture where fear is the last thing you're ever supposed to admit to. In the culture, if you project anything less than fearless confidence, you're seen as weak. Someone who is never going to make it.

That's the myth we're sold. The truth, I've come to learn, is that your favorite rapper is probably racked with as much fear as you are. Probably even more. He or she has just learned how to reckon with their fears as they continue to grow as an artist.

That's the same skill I want to teach you through this book. Facing and overcoming your fears, rather than being hand-cuffed by them.

I'm going to undress all my fears in these pages so you can see that you aren't alone in your anxieties. Not only the ones I've been aware of for years, but also the ones I've become more conscious of by going to therapy.

I've gone to therapy specifically to deal with anxiety and PTSD issues. That's been my challenge. But I also know there are a host of additional mental health issues that other people face. I want to touch on some of those too, but the truth is I'm not an expert on anyone but myself.

In order to address that, I reached out to Dr. Ish Major who is a board-certified psychiatrist. Even better, he's a black guy who got his degree from the University of South Carolina School of Medicine. After we connected, Dr. Ish agreed to write what we're calling Clinical Correlations to provide a little more detail and mental health context. The hope is that through Dr. Ish's analysis of what I've written, you'll begin to get a sense of the type of information and feedback you might get yourself through therapy.

Just to be clear, Dr. Ish is not the therapist I've been seeing. Why? Because I'm selfish. I want my therapist all to myself. I'm not trying to share her with y'all. But Dr. Ish is here for all of us. And if something he says resonates with you, I'd suggest you reach out to him directly. I've found his contributions very accessible and insightful, and I hope you will too.

I've already mentioned one classic hip-hop song, but I want to conclude by saying that in many ways this book is a response to the Mobb Deep classic "Shook Ones." Prodigy (RIP) is one of the greatest MCs of all time, and I grew up trying to live by the song's hook:

> 'Cause ain't no such things as halfway crooks
> Scared to death, scared to look, they shook. . . .
> Some get shot, locked down, and turn nuns
> Cowardly hearts and straight-up shook ones, shook ones.

However, today as a grown-ass man with a lot more experience under my belt, I have to say that way of looking at the world is bullshit.

We can be shook.

In fact, we all *should* be shook.

Because we're never going to get past our fears until we face them.

CHAPTER 2

So Anxioussssss (Ginuwine Voice)

"I had anxiety that I didn't know was anxiety. I had panic attacks that I didn't know were panic attacks. Any time I felt something I considered abnormal, I just reached for the bottle."

—DMC

I wasn't really even familiar with the term "anxiety" until about ten years ago.

At the time, I had just been fired as a radio DJ for the fourth time, which forced me to move back in with my mother in my hometown of Moncks Corner, South Carolina. My then girlfriend (now my wife, Mook Mook) had to take our daughter and move back in with her mother.

To make matters worse, I'd just spent months trying to launch the career of an unknown South Carolina rapper named Lil' Ru, only to see the deal fall apart at the last minute. I now know that's just how the music biz goes, but I was very invested in getting a South Carolina rapper to break nationally, so I took it way too personally.

I had just turned thirty-two, but it felt like I was back at square one. I hadn't hit rock bottom, but it felt like I could at any second. Was my career doing major-market radio over?

I felt tortured by my past decisions. How had everything gone so wrong?

I felt I'd done my job to the best of my ability working at 100.3 The Beat in Philly but had just gotten caught in a politics game. I damn sure didn't do anything to Lil' Ru except set him up with a great opportunity. It all didn't seem right.

I was scared for my future. I'd dreamed of being great, and now I was back living with my mama like a boy. As a man I consider it my job to protect and provide for my family, and I wasn't doing that. My dream of helping a local rapper break out and put the whole South Carolina hip-hop scene on the map was once so close but now felt like it was never going to happen (it still hasn't).

With all that trouble on my mind, I started losing it. The first time I knew something was wrong was when I was driving down Interstate 26 to go see Lil Duval perform stand-up in Orangeburg, South Carolina. My cousin Kinta was riding with me, and we were discussing all the bad things that were happening to me, when, suddenly, I started feeling light-headed.

I literally tried to shake it off, but it didn't work. Then my chest started hurting too. I knew I was in no shape to drive, so I pulled over and let Kinta take the wheel. I didn't have a word for what was happening to me, but it felt like I was experiencing a heart attack. I started praying to God to not let me die out there on the highway.

Kinta drove me to the store, where he bought me a bottle of water, and eventually I calmed down enough for us to continue. But that experience really shook me up. I thought God had spared me, and I made a vow to go see a doctor the very next day.

When I saw the doctor, he performed a bunch of tests on me and then told me, to my surprise, that my heart was fine. In fact, he said I had an athlete's heart. "What was the problem then?" I asked.

"What you probably experienced was an anxiety attack," he replied. "Ever had one before?"

"Nope," I said reflexively. "This is the first time."

He didn't give any further advice or medication. I was so relieved there was nothing wrong with my heart that I didn't press and just got out of there.

Driving home from the doctor's, however, I started leafing through my mental Rolodex. I realized that I *had* experienced those symptoms before. I just thought they were feelings that came with my lifestyle. Paranoia is a given if you're running the streets and committing crimes. I *had* feared for the future. I *had* worried that everything was going to collapse all around me. I *had* been convinced that the world was coming to an end.

I just hadn't known what to call those feelings.

Now I had a word to describe it:

Anxiety.

Hurricane Hugo

Even though I hadn't admitted it to my doctor, the truth is I had spent much of my life dealing with anxiety.

The first situation I remember getting really worried about was Hurricane Hugo. When I was eleven, we found out Hugo was going to touch down near our part of South Carolina. You might not remember it, but Hugo was a serious hurricane. I'm talking category 4, with 140-miles-an-hour winds and twenty-foot-high storm surges.

We were living in a trailer at the time, so there was no riding it out. Like most of the people on our dirt road, we went to a local school, Whitesville Elementary, and huddled in the cafeteria. My father didn't try to convince the kids that we were going on a cool sleepover. He kept it all-the-way real. He said we were facing a potential category 5 hurricane that could kill us all. Some of the adults tried to get the kids to play games or get distracted with activities, but there wasn't any fooling me. I was aware that as the wind grew louder, the older folks were low-key starting to freak out. I heard them say we'd all probably lose our trailers and houses. They said there was a chance we might not even make it through the night. I was shook.

I wasn't afraid of dying, mainly because I didn't really understand the concept yet. But I do remember the idea that we might not have a place to live once the storm was done being extremely scary.

The ancient Persians coined the adage "This too shall pass" as a way to describe the temporary nature of the human condition. What is true of humans is also true of hurricanes, because after a terrifying night Hugo finally passed by our little town.

When we ventured outside the next morning, all I wanted to know was what happened to the trailer we were living in. Would it still be there? Or were we going to have to live at the school for the rest of our lives? And outside of my own situation, I was extremely worried about my neighbors too. Would they be homeless? Was everyone going to be looking for a place to live? To an eleven-year-old kid, those were mind-blowing possibilities.

Sure enough, the aftermath of the storm revealed that a lot of folks had indeed lost their homes. On my dirt road alone there were a couple of families who had to move in with neighbors because their trailers were gone. We only had a single-wide trailer (as opposed to a more roomy double-wide), so we weren't able to take anyone in. It seemed like the only thing you heard about for the next few weeks in Moncks Corner was people struggling to survive. We were mainly poor folk who might not have had insurance, or the resources to rebuild with.

Power ended up being out for several weeks while we waited for slow-ass FEMA to do their job. I don't know what held them up, but everyone was complaining about how incompetent they were (something the people of New Orleans and Puerto Rico can attest to). I'll always remember my father saying, "FEMA isn't there for us during this hurricane, but FICA is still always taking money out of people's checks." It wasn't right, and I don't fuck with neither of them to this day!

Most kids take things like their home, clothes, and toys for granted, but Hurricane Hugo taught me a different reality. I became hyperconscious that none of those things were promised. And that unsettled feeling, the sense that your life could literally be blown away, became very hard for me to shake. Seeing the enormity of all that destruction made me aware of the possibility of death for the first time. When I saw how all those trees snapped like toothpicks and cars had gotten flipped over like toys, then I knew I wouldn't have stood a chance out in the open.

As I grew a little older, my anxiety began to manifest itself in different ways.

Like most young people, I could get very anxious about fitting in. Having a seat at the cool table. Especially in middle school, I was very confused about my social standing. I was hanging out with a bunch of white kids, but I could never tell how they really felt about me. We seemed cool at school, but I would never get invited over to hang out or to their birthday parties.

On the other hand were my thugged-out cousins. I knew I could definitely fit in with them if I wanted to, but I hated hanging out with them. They were nothin' but bad news, and I didn't want to deal with the peer pressure to get into trouble. Remember that TLC song "What About Your Friends"?

What about your friends, will they stand their ground?
Will they let you down again?

Those were literally the questions that seemed to be stuck on a steady loop in my head during my teenage years.

No matter how many times I was offered a seat at the cool kids' table, I never really felt secure in my social status. But by far my greatest source of anxiety growing up was whether my peers thought I was "pussy." To avoid that, I had to be hardcore. A thug. A gangsta. Someone who gave zero fucks.

It was an attitude and lifestyle copied from our favorite rappers and actors. This was the nineties, and for us, songs like Onyx's "Throw Ya Gunz," Redman's "Time 4 Sum Aksion," or Cypress Hill's "How I Could Just Kill a Man," weren't just music, they were closer to an audio bible. Words that we studied, revered, and tried to live by.

Same with movies. We worshipped Tupac's character "Bishop" in *Juice* and Lorenz Tate's "O-Dog" in *Menace II Society*. It's impossible to overstate the impact these movies had on us. I literally went out and bought a Model 64 Smith & Wesson .38 special because that's what Tupac carried in *Juice*. I was desperate to have people fear me the way they feared Bishop. It seemed like he had power! I wanted some too. I yearned to have the same reputation—fearless, reckless, and dangerous.

Guns were the ultimate sign of recklessness, but we were pretty loose with our fists too. Among my friends, the most important way to prove you weren't pussy was always being willing to use your hands. See a random white boy walking down the hallway at school? Punch him in the face. Crackhead owe us some money? Let's jump him! (Being the one who threw the first punch was always important.) Some nigga you don't like at school because he may get more chicks than you? Or got better gear than you? Then start a fight with him, snuff him! Scum-bag hater shit, I know, but, hey, we felt like those were things our hard-core heroes would have done. No matter what the situation, we were always looking for an excuse to fight. Someone look at you the wrong way? Time to "bam" (our slang for fighting). Someone step on your new Timbs? Time to bam too. Everyone sitting around bored with nothing to do? Then it's time for two of us to square up.

One time I was hanging out on Highway 6 with a few of my folks when Darnell pulled up. Yes, the same Darnell who beat my ass in the intro of *Black Privilege* and almost Diddy-cropped me out of life. Knowing what it was like to be on the receiving end of one of his choke holds, I had an instant panic attack just seeing him. To the point where I couldn't even move. I was standing still, hoping to disappear. In my mind, if I stood there long enough I might be able to fade back into the bushes, the way Homer Simpson does in that GIF everyone uses. Of course it didn't happen. Instead, Darnell saw me plain as day and immediately wanted to fight. My boy, who's nickname was Neck, then asked Darnell, "Do you want to shoot a fair one with 'Nard?" Darnell immediately said, "Let's go." I might have been tough smacking crackheads and white boys, but I didn't want any smoke with Darnell. The last time he'd whipped my ass it was only his two cousins who witnessed it. I didn't want to take the same sort of beating in front of my boys. Trouble was, I also didn't want them to think I was pussy by backing down from the challenge. I knew I was taking an "L" either way. My boys were going to think I was pussy, or Darnell was going to beat me down.

Ultimately I didn't really have a choice because every fiber in my body could remember the last beating and started screaming, "Nigga, no! Do not fight him!" I couldn't have moved my feet even if I had wanted to. Somehow I got my mouth to work and respectfully declined his offer.

I wasn't willing to risk getting killed by guys like Darnell because I knew deep down I had very little in common with a Bishop or an O-Dog. Every time I punched a white boy in the face or tucked a .38 into my goose jacket, it was only to mask that I was in fact *extremely* pussy.

I'd been like that since I was a kid. There were countless times I'd go hide in the woods surrounding Moncks Corner rather than run the chance of bumping into the so-called tough guy. Oh, I was late to many a class, taking the long way in middle school or ducking off in a bathroom stall, desperate to avoid a tough nigga who might have it in for me.

I still distinctly remember back in sixth grade I let an eighth grader named JT borrow my "Kung Fu" Nintendo game. He was supposed to give it back the next day, but a week later I still didn't have my game. When I finally did see him, using the toughest-sounding voice I could muster, I demanded, "Hey, JT, you promised to give me my game back. Hand it over!" JT just laughed and walked right by me. I didn't have it in me to chase him down and fight for what was mine. After that I was basically reduced to begging him to give me my game back. It got to a point that even just the mention of this guy's name would flood my mind with nervousness and unease. Finally one of my older neighbors, Reggie President, decided to put an end to my humiliation. (It wasn't so much that Reggie felt sorry for me, but more that he wanted to play the game himself. When you live on a dirt road, being short even one video game is a big deal.) "You still didn't get your 'Kung Fu' back? You gotta stop being so pussy," Reggie said to me, shaking his head. And then he went and tracked down JT and retrieved the game without incident.

Things got even worse when I entered Berkeley High School. That school was so bad that it resembled a *Lean on Me* situation. The district realized they had to bring in a whole new administration just to clean up the mess some of the students created.

Even though I had played a major role in creating the chaos, I was still always nervous about being forced into a fight. That might seem like a perfectly normal way to feel (after all, who but an MMA fighter wants to go around getting punched every day?), but at the time I had to carry it around like a dark secret. Like I'm sure a lot of other brothers and sisters in the school were.

The situation came to a head the February of my junior year

of high school. Without warning, I suddenly found myself unable to defend myself whenever I got into a fight. Which was a problem, because within the space of a few weeks I got into several scrapes. Each time, I couldn't lift my hands to defend myself. Guys were punching me in the face, and I just took it. My cousin Aaron beat me up. Not too long later I got washed up by Darnell. Then a guy name Kendrick hit me in the face with a lock because of some girl. All within a couple of weeks. Each time it felt like there was nothing I could do. At the time, I convinced myself that a spell (or as we call it down South, "roots") had been put on me so that I couldn't fight back.

At the end of that month I decided to go see *Set It Off* with a chick I was dating at the time. It was one of our first dates, but I had to wear an eye patch, due to a black eye I had received from getting hit with the lock. Thank God Slick Rick was a legend to us, so the eye patch didn't look too awkward. The theater was packed, and it seemed like every "hard-core" person in a thirty-mile radius was there. All I could think about was someone sneaking up behind me in the dark and then snuffing me out in front of my date. Everyone in the theater was loving the movie, but I could barely concentrate on the screen. I kept looking around with my one good eye to see if someone was creeping on me. Before I knew it, I was in a full-blown panic attack.

The darkness provided me a little cover, and I tried to take a few minutes to calm myself down. It was no use. Finally I couldn't take it anymore and told my date we had to leave, even though the movie was barely halfway done. She didn't understand why, but to her credit she didn't complain and left with me. It would be months before I found out that Queen Latifah's character, Cleo, and Vivica A. Fox's character, Frankie, died at the end of the movie! (If that was a spoiler, I'm not sorry. It's your fucking fault for never having seen *Set It Off*!)

My anxiety got even worse as I got a little older and started to dabble in selling drugs. Imagine standing on the street with a vial of crack in your pocket and every time a car pulls up, you're not sure whether it's a sale or cops trying to bust the block. It was hell.

Not that we were doing ourselves any favors. My father used to call us sitting ducks and remind us that smart drug dealers don't keep still; they move around. "You are just sitting there waiting for something bad to happen, and eventually it will. You think police don't know you sitting back in that hole hustling? Eventually they are coming for you!" We knew he was right, which put some serious fear in our hearts.

It was the same with other guys who were really out there in the streets. Hustlers you'd always see with the fly cars, clothes, and "hoes." Yes, they had all the toys to make folks envious, but they also had serious paranoia, panic, and angst that people couldn't see. They always kept a gun on them because they were worried about being robbed. They never spoke on the phone because they were nervous about the police listening in. They always drove the speed limit when they were on the road so cops didn't have an excuse to pull them over. The whole hustler lifestyle was nothing but worry and uncertainty.

There weren't a lot of places I could turn to for help dealing with my fears. I couldn't really talk to my parents about it, because my parents were more concerned about the anxiety I was causing *them* by selling drugs. In their minds, it probably would have been a pretty simple solution: if you're anxious about getting in fights or being arrested by the police, then stop hanging out with thugs and dealing drugs!

Great advice, but it would have also meant coming out as pussy, which is probably why I never opened up to my parents about what I was experiencing emotionally.

My father in particular didn't want to hear about me being anxious. If my father had found me hiding in the woods one of those times, he would have asked, "Boy, what the hell you doin' out here in these damn woods?"

And if I told him the truth, "I was scared of seeing this kid Bobby. He's been mean to me," his head would have exploded. Our fathers probably knew each other, and if I was scared of Bobby, then that meant his pop's had one up on mine. That would have been unacceptable to my father.

"Scared?" he would have yelled. "Scared of that punk! Get out from under this tree and go whup his ass before I whup yours!" Back then, telling my father I was scared would have been the same as telling him I was gay. He just didn't want to hear it.

If we had been a little more aware of the signs, however, we might have noticed that there was definitely a streak of paranoia running through my family. Looking back, I can see that my grandmother in particular had terrible anxiety. She used to go on and on about how people were about to come out of the woods surrounding her house and take her away. She also would tell us how her late husband would visit her in dreams and he would warn her about bad things that were about to happen to us. At the time, I considered it almost comical how wrapped up she was. I even stopped visiting her as much because I thought she was too pessimistic about things and "bringing me down." I wish I had the knowledge back then to have been more understanding of what she was going through.

These days you could call me pussy at the top of your lungs

and I wouldn't even flinch. I don't care anymore when it comes to my masculinity. You know what's masculine? Masculine is taking care of your mind, your body, and your soul. We spend so much time on our body. We want that six-pack. We gotta have big biceps. We take all sorts of pills when we start losing our hair. But what about our mental health? What about our emotional well-being? I go to the gym three, four times a week. Why can't I put that same effort and same energy into getting mentally strong? If that makes me pussy, then I'm going to stay pussy for the rest of my life.

The Power of Perception

As I've grown older, I've found some of my biggest fears come from my insecurities. Specifically those rooted in what I *perceive* to be other people's opinions of me. My issue was never with *being* pussy. Only with being *perceived* that way.

Anxiety almost always lives in our perceptions, not our reality. This has probably been the case since the beginning of time. Some prehistoric caveman was afraid to come out to the communal campfire because his club (dick) wasn't as big as the guy who lived a few caves down. Probably the reason pants were invented. When all the other cavemen saw the first guy with a club hanging to his knees, they must have gotten a complex about their own situations. Someone started grunting instructions for someone to take two bear pelts and sew them together into some pants just so they wouldn't have to be intimidated by the sight of that long-ass club all day!

I know the power of perception was a problem back in the days of slavery too. Take the relationship between the house

21

and field Negroes. When Massa showed more love and affection to the house Negroes, those field Negroes would feel inferior and burn with envy. But guess what? It shouldn't have mattered, because even if one brother was sleeping in the big house while the other was out in a little hut, at the end of the day they were both STILL SLAVES. Neither of them was leaving that plantation of their own volition without getting a bullet in their back.

Those damn colonizers didn't limit their plots to house versus field Negroes either. They pitted old versus young, dark skin against light skin, and men against women. That was because the slave masters rightly figured that as long as they could keep us Africans fighting among one another, we would never unify and threaten the establishment of slavery. Better for us to forever hate each other than to turn that fury toward our massa! (Sound familiar? It should, because those artificial divisions are still the number one cause of a lot of insecurity and jealousy in the African-American community today!)

If those slaves had been able to get on the same page and work together, then maybe they could have put a bullet in Massa's back instead. And then today we wouldn't still have to be dealing with the white devils who run the system trying to gaslight our fears.

The Impact of Social Media

Insecurity and jealousy may always have been a part of our makeup, but social media has amplified their powers to heights that our ancestors would never have dreamed possible.

Take my middle school nickname, "Boonky Nose." ("Boonky" was slang for butt.) I didn't have a perception people thought my nose was big—they called me "Boonky Nose" to my face almost every day. I felt a way about it for a little while, but eventually I was able to get past the taunts and embrace having a sizable snout.

I might not have been able to shrug it off quite so easily though if social media had been around back then. Imagine if my classmates at Berkeley Middle School had had access to Photoshop. They would have made some of the greatest memes on the planet at my expense. I'm imagining images of my face photoshopped on pictures of Toucan Sam, Snuffleupagus, and my favorite, Mr. Magoo (not the rapper, the little half-blind, big-nosed cartoon character). Those images would have ripped on the internet back in the day!

Man, there is no way that my younger self could have handled a constant onslaught of online slander. When you are a young, impressionable kid whose mind is still being shaped, you need constant positive reinforcement. Not negative garbage thrown at you by thousands, potentially millions, of strangers. And as a father, I get extremely scared every time I read about online bullying causing a young kid to commit suicide. I don't like to even think about those situations, but they're real.

I'm a grown-ass man, and even though I know better, I still take internet slander personal at times. I think it's because when I was growing up you had to deal with the consequences of your words. I thought that's how things were supposed to work. Nowadays complete strangers can just talk trash to you from anywhere in the world without you getting the chance to hold them accountable. It's very frustrating. I literally have to remind myself these digital dickheads don't know me, they just want me to reply to the hate they send my way, because misery absolutely loves company.

I've heard it all online. That I hate black women. That I pander to black women. That I'm an Uncle Tom. That I hate white people. That I'm gay. That I'm homophobic. How can I be all those things simultaneously? It's almost impossible! (I say "almost" because there are plenty of Republican politicians who have shown that it is possible to be gay and homophobic at the same time.)

People don't care about the truth on social media when a lie is much more entertaining. For instance, a few years ago a picture started circulating of a butt-naked, bald-headed, brown-skinned, boonky-nosed dude facedown on all fours. This guy was staring straight at the camera while busting his boy pussy wide-open for the world to see! Somehow social media decided it was a picture of me. Why, I'll never know.

Yes, I've been seeing a dermatologist (the great Dr. Natasha Sandy) for a while now, but she doesn't do ass injections. So just off this dude's fat ass you know it wasn't a picture of me. The only thing me and this guy in the picture got in common is a bald head, skin complexion, and boonky nose. But apparently that's enough for the internet. Whenever folks get caught up in a "let's cancel Charlamagne" moment, someone will inevitably drag up this photo and send it to me with a post saying, "I knew you were gay!" or, "Charlamagne is a bottom!"

My favorite is when people will forward me the pic with the simple caption: "Explain!"

"Explain what?" I want to respond. "Explain why you're sending me a picture of another man butt-naked down on all fours? Isn't that a question that you need to ask yourself?"

You shouldn't have to explain a lie on social media when you already know the truth about a situation. You should be able to simply say, "That's not me," or even "That's not what I meant," and then keep it moving. Why isn't this enough for us? It shouldn't matter if other people know the truth when we know the truth about ourselves. But that's not how it works, is it? Our own anxiety, our own personal insecurities, want to clap back and "set the record straight." But guess what: swinging at online spirits never works!

I call this phenomenon "trying to punch a ghost," because if you swing with all your might, and even seem to connect, you're never going to hit anything! If anything, you will only end up exhausting yourself and maybe even breaking your hand because your fist might go through the ghost and hit a wall. So before you start throwing emotional haymakers, ask yourself, "Why do I care about the opinions of people who don't know me? Why do I care about lies that I know aren't true?" Whenever you feel yourself wanting to swing back at people online, remind yourself: "I'm not Pac-Man. I don't need to chase ghosts!"

The truth needs no defense, only witnesses, and the greatest witness you have is yourself! Why get insecure and anxious when you KNOW THE TRUTH. You know the rumors, gossip, and bullshit people are spreading about you online isn't real, so why do you care so much?

The Tomi Tsunami

You can post pictures of me next to Sammy Sosa all day and I'll barely pay it any mind. Make fun of my nose, or how short

I am, and I'll probably laugh right along with you. Send me a picture of another man naked, and I might wonder why'd you do it, but I won't waste a second worrying about it.

There are, however, jabs thrown my way on social media that still hurt me. Primarily ones targeting my craft. As much as I'd like to say I'm above it, if you write something negative about me as a media personality, or about *The Breakfast Club* or *The Brilliant Idiots*, or how I've conducted an interview, it's going to get under my skin. Because, if I'm being honest, despite all the success and praise I've enjoyed, that's still the aspect of my life I'm the most insecure about. When Erykah Badu sang, "Now keep in mind I'm an artist / and I'm sensitive about my shit," I could relate. I feel that way about my craft as well.

I've produced many a media firestorm over things I've said, and they never fail to stress me all the way out. Which is ironic, because the tweets or comments I've made that have ignited those storms were never intended to be inflammatory. People might think I say things just to get a reaction, but I promise it's not so. I've never hit "post" on a tweet, rubbed my hands together Birdman-style, and thought, "Good, now that's going to get my mentions lit!" No, the tweets that have caused me the most drama are the ones I never thought would make much of an impact. It's terrible to not be able to predict if a tweet is going to cause a full-on Twitter tsunami. It's stressful.

One great example of this is a tweet I sent out in 2016 about the conservative media personality Tomi Lahren. If you're not familiar, Tomi is a blue-eyed, blond-haired, mayonnaise-loving host for Fox News, who is also the very definition of a troll. Meaning, she does things just to get a reaction out of people. Especially African-Americans.

Tomi first appeared on my radar back in the winter of 2016, when several people hit me up on social media to say I needed to give her Donkey of the Day, the award I hand out on *The Breakfast Club* to people who have made asses of themselves. Tomi had riled them up (probably intentionally) by denouncing Beyoncé's Super Bowl halftime performance as "anti-police" because it paid homage to the Black Panther Party.

I hadn't heard of her, but when I listened to her comments I found plenty that would make her an excellent Donkey candidate. She had indeed disrespected the legacy of the Black Panthers by falsely claiming they advocated violence over peace. She'd also disrespected Beyoncé by pointing out that her husband, Jay-Z, used to be a drug dealer (which was true, but what does it have to do with the man he's become? and the man Beyoncé married?). So I gave Tomi a well-earned Donkey and figured that would be the end of it.

Far from it. Almost immediately after giving Tomi a "hee-haw," her former network TheBlaze asked me if I wanted to come on her show and have a debate about Beyoncé and the Black Panthers. Some folks might have said, "Why even give her that much attention?" But I had no problem doing it. TheBlaze was founded by the conservative media personality Glenn Beck and I figured going on there would let me reach a lot of right-wing viewers who otherwise would probably never hear from someone with my POV. Why wouldn't I embrace the opportunity to change some people's minds who have been fed a lot of bad information? I know that right-wingers seem entrenched in their views, but I refuse to believe they're unmovable when confronted with logical truth. I believe false narratives can always be turned into teachable moments. Those people weren't going to get correct information about Beyoncé and the Black Panthers unless I stepped into their living rooms and brought it to them.

So I went on Tomi's show and calmly explained that Beyoncé's Super Bowl performance wasn't an anti-police performance but rather an anti–police *brutality* performance. A big difference. Then I informed her that the Black Panthers were not a hate group or a domestic terrorist organization like the KKK, but rather did a lot of positive things for African-American communities, like providing free lunch programs and keeping the people safe from corrupt police officers.

TheBlaze ended up editing the fuck out of that video. (They were probably trying to obscure the fact Tomi didn't know what she was talking about. Too bad they couldn't edit her appearances on *The Daily Show with Trevor Noah* or on *Real Time with Bill Maher* too. . . .) I still managed to get a few good points out. I have to believe at least a few people were able to look at Beyoncé and the Black Panthers differently. Probably even more would have if TheBlaze had aired the unedited version. My man DJ Akademics went as far as to post it on his YouTube page, which resulted in TheBlaze getting it pulled down from various websites that reposted it. It's still out there somewhere though, if you want to see it.

Despite their trickery, her team asked if she could be on *The Breakfast Club*, and I said absolutely, because I knew this time I wouldn't end up on the editing room floor. We agreed to do it the morning after she taped *The Daily Show*. Unfortunately Trevor Noah made her sound so foolish (my favorite moment was when she said, "I don't see color," and he shot back, "So what do you do at a traffic light?") that her handlers panicked and canceled on us the next morning.

An executive over at Viacom, who's a great friend of mine named Paul Ricci, was kicking around the idea of a debate-style TV show between Tomi and me. Paul's my guy, but I never really liked the concept; in fact, I said if anyone should be doing a debate show with her, it should be a liberal woman of color. That way both sides are represented. I agreed to take the meeting anyway, mainly because I was interested in seeing if she was just portraying a character on TV, or if this was really where her head was at.

During the meeting, I tried to explain to Tomi why her rhetoric is dangerous to the black community. In particular, I wanted to know why she said the Black Lives Matter movement was an anti-police organization that supported violence toward cops.

Her response was she had been in Dallas the night several officers were killed during a BLM march and she had heard protesters chanting that they wanted to kill cops. She also told me that BLM protestors had sent both her and her parents death threats and even put their address online, which really scared her.

"Fair enough," I responded. "But let me ask you something. Are you a Trump supporter?"

Tomi said that she was.

"Do you think all Trump supporters are racist?" I asked her.

"No," she replied. "I know some of the folks at his rallies are racist, but I think the vast majority of them are like me, people who are tired of government as usual and want a change."

"So why is it you can see the nuance in Trump supporters but can't see the nuance in people who say they are BLM?" I asked her. "BLM wasn't built on violence toward law enforcement, it was about stopping police brutality. So if you have a few people who identify as BLM chanting they want to kill cops, why would you paint the whole organization with that false narrative? That's exactly like me saying all Trump supporters are racist" (which may or may not be the case, by the way).

Paul and Tomi's two agents who were also in the room all said it was a great point and then looked to Tomi to make some sort of concession. But she refused to acknowledge my point. "Not the same," she insisted. It was then I decided she was either really committed to her character or just really dumb.

After the meeting, we took a pic together that I posted on Instagram in black-and-white with the caption "Do you see color?" (A play on what she had said to Trevor.) Also, after the meeting, TMZ caught us coming out of the Viacom office and asked us what we were doing. I said that we were having a conversation and it was important for people who don't agree to still share a dialogue (which I do believe, whatever I thought of Tomi). And that was the last time I saw Tomi Lahren. I didn't take her to lunch, dinner, coffee, drinks, or any other lie social media came up with later on. And even though she was never on *The Breakfast Club* (she only got an invite) or my podcast *The Brilliant Idiots*, or any of my TV shows, to this day people will see me and say, "Stop having Tomi Lahren on your show!!!" Ummmmm . . .

In the coming weeks I couldn't help but notice that she was continuing to make a lot of noise on social media, especially on Facebook. Her rhetoric was terrible, but she had taken the platform TheBlaze had given her and then made it even bigger by talking about us. And by us, I mean Black Twitter. Tomi might not be the freshest jar of mayo in the refrigerator, but she was smart enough to realize that black folks set the temperature online. If we decide something needs to be discussed, it's only a matter of time before it becomes the national conversation. Whether it's supporting someone or slandering them, if we decide to engage, the whole country will follow.

Tomi cashed in on that cache. She would say something wild, Black Twitter would go in on her, and she'd start trending. Then her supporters would rush into the conversation to defend her, and before you knew it: *boom!* She'd created a media storm that only served to raise her profile.

Once I realized what she was up to, I wanted to figure out a way to take that power away from her and give it back to the people who had created it in the first place: *Black Twitter*. I wanted to see one of the voices from Black Twitter get a platform as big as Tomi's. I'd also been watching several shows on the political network The Young Turks and wanted to see a woman of color create something similar.

With that thought in mind, I sent out the following tweet:

Would be dope if a young black or Hispanic "WOKE" woman used social media to create a Platform to be a voice like Tomi Lahren did.

The sentiment behind that tweet, I promise you, was very pure. What was messy, unfortunately, was my lack of articulation. By framing the statement as it "would be dope *if*," I implied that there weren't any females doing it. What I should have done, in retrospect, was frame my statement as a question: "Who are the young black or Hispanic woke women out there with platforms that we can empower?" That way we could directly uplift them, instead of indirectly uplifting someone like Tomi.

31

Had I done that, I believe the tweet would have immediately ignited a conversation about all the incredible women on social media who are moving the culture forward in that political-pundit-type space. Women who I was not only familiar with and in many cases worked with but who also, I felt, hadn't received the attention they deserved.

But that's not what happened. Instead, I framed the tweet as "Would be dope if . . ." and immediately things spun out of control. The narrative became "Charlamagne wants women of color to be like Tomi Lahren" before quickly escalating to "Charlamagne hates black women." Mind you, I never even remotely said either of those things, but once a narrative starts building, it's tough to slow it down.

When a Twitter storm starts burning that hot, there's nothing to do except own that you fucked up. Yes, my intentions were good and I felt my tweet had been misinterpreted. But I'm a professional communicator, and if I can't communicate what I'm trying to express in a clear fashion, then that's on me. That's why the very next morning I gave myself Donkey of the Day, because I had definitely made an ass out of myself.

The Donkey might have been well deserved, but Twitter wasn't going to let me live that tweet down. No matter how many times I acknowledged and apologized for my mistake. Even up to this day, whenever I say something even remotely questionable, people will send me that tweet, usually with a caption like, "See, there goes Charlamagne hating on black women again."

SO ANXIOUSSSSSSS (GINUWINE VOICE)

F.E.A.R

> Not everything that is faced can be changed. But
> nothing can be changed until it is faced.
> —James Baldwin

That tweet caused me a lot of stress, but do I regret it? Not even
a little bit. The great radio personality and my homie K.Foxx
once told me, "You have to look at F-E-A-R as having two
meanings: 'forget everything and run,' or 'face everything and
rise.'"

As K explained it, that means when a situation makes you
anxious, don't run from it. Or make excuses. Instead, your best
recourse is always to face it head-on. Confront any insecurities
that might have been behind your actions and then try to fix
them. Once you have, dust yourself off and continue to rise in
your journey.

And that's ultimately what happened to me after the Tomi
text. Yes, I took a bad beating on social media. But I also
learned a lot about the incredible work women of color were
already doing on social media. Work that has really enhanced
my understanding of politics and social issues.

Perhaps most important, that situation also led to me
becoming better friends with my spiritual sister, the übertal-
ented political commenter Angela Rye. Angela was one of the
main people Twitter told me was already building platforms
and doing work. To her credit, instead of being insulted by
my ignorance, Angela reached out to me with real empathy. "I
understood what you were trying to say," she tweeted me. "But
it definitely didn't come out right."

That's all my dumb ass needed: someone smarter than me

who understood what I was trying to say and instead of crushing me, pointed me in the right direction. Angela has the type of voice I was trying to call for in that tweet. My man Van Lathan of TMZ calls her the "Warrior Goddess of Woke" and that phrase couldn't be more accurate. I love nothing more than watching her destroy colonizers on CNN, obliterate white devils on social media, and keep the *Breakfast Club* audience on point with what I call her monthly state of the unions. She's one of the best strategists I know and always has a plan to make something positive happen for black people. So even though I still get little anxiety pangs whenever someone brings up that tweet, getting the connection with Angela makes up for the category 5 tsunami that came after it.

Life Before the Internet

So much of the anxiety we feel today is rooted in social media. In fact, I guarantee social media is the number one cause of anxiety on the planet. In theory, it's there to help us stay connected. In reality, however, it often ends up making us feel alone and even depressed. We can lose a lot of that self-inflicted stress if we can remember that we were able to survive—not to mention thrive—without it.

It might shock millennials to hear this, but I still can remember what it was like before our lives ran through our phones and we were actually able to find our way around without Google Maps or Waze. We'd have to figure out where we were going by observing the landscape and sometimes just getting lost. Someone might say, "Drive on East Main Street, past Howards, keep going till you see the First Baptist Church and then turn left on South Live Oak Drive. Keep driving till you see a big field and then the house will be just after it on the right." Directions like that forced us to *pay attention*. Maybe we'd make a few wrong turns and eventually pull over to the side of the road and look at a map or ask directions at a gas station, but we'd get to where we had to go.

We also didn't have the internet to take the place of our memory. We had to actually learn and memorize things, which wasn't always fun, but I can still tell you about a history report I wrote in ninth grade. (And we made stuff with our hands. In the ninth grade I made a Captain Caveman club in home-ed class and carried it around school with me for protection. No one could say anything because I'd made it in school.)

Research meant time in a library, not on your phone. And you know what happens when you spend hours in a library? You end up reading books. Maybe even books you weren't expecting to be interesting, or those outside your life experience.

If you wanted to call a friend, or your mother, you had to have those phone numbers memorized. You didn't have your entire contact list at your fingertips. I bet most people reading this right now don't know their mother's phone number by heart. That would have been unthinkable back in the day.

Those might seem like small points, but collectively they made our brains stronger! All those tasks, directions, challenges, and problems acted as mental exercises. The type that we aren't getting anymore. As a result, our brain muscles are getting soft.

But much more important than having to figure out how to read a map or calculate sales tax, back in the day before social media we used to do things together. In person. Face-to-face instead of on FaceTime.

The god Raekwon Da Chef once rapped, "It's for real though, let's connect politic—ditto!" Those words still resonate with me over twenty years later because that's what our lives revolved around back then. "Politic" was slang for physically getting together with your people and kicking it. You would link up, maybe roll a few blunts, and start "building." That was slang for having a real, in-depth discussion about a topic. Or depending on how many blunts got rolled, multiple topics. It was a critical way for us to learn about things from our peers and develop our philosophies on life.

While there's plenty of political debate happening on social media, there's not nearly enough "politicking" going on anymore. Young people don't seem interested in having conversations in person these days.

I used to spend hours with my crew sitting on porches, hanging out in basements, or chillin' by the ball fields while we argued over everything under the sun. Whether my cousin really asked that cute girl in science class out on a date. Whether Mobb Deep was better than Outkast. How Magic managed to keep playing with AIDS. Whether Tupac was still alive.

You might start out arguing with one person, but it was only a matter of time before everyone else would jump in and add their two cents. If you made a good point, you might get cheers and pounds. If you said something wack or told a joke that fell flat, you would definitely get clowned. Those politicking sessions made you feel like a verbal gladiator stepping into the arena. You had to learn how to bring the heat, or get scorched yourself. Those countless hours taught me to be a more confident public speaker. There's no way I would have succeeded in media without that trial by fire.

I also enjoyed listening to great speakers and storytellers. One of the reasons I started studying the Five Percenter teachings of Islam was because of the authority those brothers spoke with in front of a crowd. I aspired to be that articulate. To possess knowledge, wisdom, and understanding of myself and to be able to share it with others. The type of authority you can never convey through a text or a post.

To truly reach people, you have to keep your mental sword sharp. Unfortunately, social media is no way to hone a blade. It's mostly one-way conversations. Ironically this is why I sometimes miss dealing drugs. I don't miss running from the cops, worrying about getting robbed by other dealers, or knowing I was damaging my community. But I do miss, if I'm being honest, the camaraderie. I didn't play any organized sports growing up. Only hustling gave me the bond that comes with a group of people being together and playing for the same team. Facing the same obstacles together. My crew and I ate together, made runs to the store together, fought together, got drunk and high together, and played cat and mouse with the cops together. Through all of that we kept up a running conversation in which we discussed women, politics, clothes, TV, movies, comics, our families, and since more than a few of us were wannabe rappers, even ideas for songs. We also talked each other off the ledge when it came to acts we felt went too far, like committing armed robberies. The things we bonded over might not have all been positive, but there's no denying the strength of the connection.

I'm sorry, but you can't get that sort of bond from a group chat. I'm on some fire group chats, but they couldn't even remotely match the bond I experienced with my crew. Physically sharing an experience just takes things to another level.

Young people today prefer to text when they communicate with each other, but I think that is going to come back to haunt them. If you're going to do everything through your phone, at least call people and hear their voices. Having conversations for hours with our friends on the phone was pivotal in building social skills. All those bills we rang up waxing poetic to the ladies strengthened our ability to communicate our feelings, desires, and dreams. Skills that are necessary to evolve into a mature and happy adult. There's no way texting emojis and GIFs can improve your ability to communicate with other people. You can't fully express how you're feeling in a relationship with emojis. Just like you're not going to be able to use GIFs and emojis in a job interview (and if you are, then we're probably all screwed).

I've had a gut feeling for the last several years that social media is getting in the way of people making true, lasting connections. Now the science is backing me up. According to *Psychology Today*:

> *A new study from the University of Oxford reaffirms the importance of cultivating and nurturing friendships with face-to-face contact. The researchers found that using social media exclusively to interact with close friends may inadvertently cause the bonds of these friendships to weaken.**

*Christopher Bergland. "Maintaining Close Friendships Requires Face-to-Face Contact," *Psychology Today*, January 19, 2016, psychologytoday.com /us/blog/the-athletes-way/201601/maintaining-close-friendships-requires -face-face-contact.

The article goes on to say that although people have many more "friends" now, thanks to social media, they actually have less people they think they could turn to in a crisis, or lean on for emotional support. Sue Fudge, one of the study's authors, adds,

> *Although social media may seem like the perfect way to make and maintain friendships, this research shows that face-to-face interaction is essential for truly authentic relationships, and that shares, selfies, and "likes" are no replacement for the bonding that takes place whilst sharing food, experiences, and anecdotes.*

Amen.

I'm not saying that everyone needs a crew of drug dealers to create those bonds with, but you do need a crew that you can build with—IN PERSON.

That's why I'm trying to make a concerted effort to do more activities with my friends face-to-face. One way is having people over for dinner and letting them spend time with my family. That's something I was hesitant to do in the past, but I'm realizing that attitude was counterproductive. There's a real bond that's built when families interact. It's very important for generations to mix so that lessons can be handed down. Hanging out with other like-minded families is how I want my kids to learn how to socialize, cook, laugh, dance, and love. Not by watching some stranger do them online.

Hanging out with people is critical. There is nothing I love more than a Red Cup kickback with friends and family. They provide my family a much more realistic sense of how people live than being on-line. To have social media tell it, everyone looks great, wears fashionable clothes, drives nice cars, takes vacations to amazing places, and is always surrounded by beautiful people. As my Moncks Corner brother Pastor Steven Furtick says regarding the dangers of social media, "One reason we struggle with insecurity: we're comparing our behind the scenes to everyone else's highlight reel."

When we spend countless hours each week scrolling through people's IG and Facebook accounts, our own lives can start to feel very insignificant, or uninspiring, by comparison. As we start to get further into the social media age, studies are beginning to prove what a lot of us have already been saying.

In Denmark, researchers found that frequent users begin to develop what they call "Facebook envy." Essentially, they get so caught up in the fun other people seem to be having on Facebook that their ability to enjoy their own lives begins to decline. Over time, that envy begins to morph into depression and decreased life satisfaction.

Not surprisingly, the study found when the participants stayed off Facebook for just a week, their emotions became much more positive and their satisfaction in their own lives increased.

The connection between unhappiness and social media is particularly strong among teenagers. A study for the American Psychological Association found evidence that the more time teens spent on social media, the less happy they were. "We found that teens who spent more time seeing their friends in person, exercising, playing sports, attending religious services, reading or even doing homework were happier," said Jean Twenge, a professor of psychology at San Diego State, in an article for *Vice*. "However, teens who spent more time on the internet, playing computer games, on social media, texting, using video chat or watching TV were less happy."

The study had bad news for adults too. According to Professor Twenge, adults over the age of thirty are less happy than they were fifteen years ago. To compound that (or maybe because of it) those adults are also having less sex. While the author admits that there could be several factors behind the decrease in happiness, there's no doubt that it's connected to the fact that adults are spending more time than ever on screens.

Professor Twenge says that for teenagers, it's important that they limit the time they spend on their phones. That's because teens who spend more than five hours a day on smartphones are 71 percent more likely to develop risk factors for suicide. That's a really scary number. Professor Twenge says the ideal amount of time for teens to spend on phones every day is between a half hour and an hour. Even up to two hours can be OK. But once a teen starts spending over three hours a day on their phone, it can be a serious threat to their mental health.

Addicted to Algorithms

I can talk all day about not basing your love life on swipes, or the importance of creating relationships that aren't exclusive to your phone, but I also concede that's often easier said than done. That's because most of us, to some degree or another, suffer from a form of addiction to social media. And like any addiction, it can bring a tremendous amount of stress and anxiety into your life.

On a scale of one to Whitney and Bobby in the nineties, I personally fall closer to "I get high a little more than I should" than "straight-up crackhead." I still definitely have a problem though.

I'm never going to completely break my dependency on phones, which I've accepted are a necessary evil. Especially when you have a family. There are a lot of instances where I need to communicate with my wife and children, and obviously a cell phone makes that much easier. One of the reasons I love going on vacation is because when I have my entire family physically around me, then I don't need my phone anymore. There's no emergency or sudden change in plans that I need to be alerted to. When we go to the beach, I leave my phone in the safe in our room. I'll feel the urge to check my texts, or my mentions on Twitter, but spending time with the people I love is a stronger motivation, and I get past it. I've found that when I'm on vacation I can wean myself off my phone for at least a few hours at a time, which allows me to focus my attention where it belongs.

My day-to-day life, however, is a different story. It's still a struggle for me to stay off my phone for more than a few minutes. I have my phone in my hand a lot of times for no reason at all. Like taking it into the bathroom when I go pee. That's right, I pee with my phone in my left hand and dick in my right. For what? Just so I can scroll through social media for fifteen seconds? Don't get me wrong, Twitter on the shitter is acceptable, because that's like reading a book or a magazine. But Twitter while peeing? That's when you know you're a broadband basehead.

One time I actually dropped my phone in the toilet while I was peeing. As soon as I fished it out, I put it in a bag of rice, because, for some strange reason, that is a home remedy that really works when you drop your phone in water. I used that method twice and still used the rice. Even after I dropped the phone in the toilet. My brilliant-idiot logic tells me the boiling water will kill the germs, so why waste perfectly good rice?

Even after drying the phone in the rice, I still needed to wait till the next morning to take it into the store to get it looked at. Those hours without my phone felt like agony.

I've never had a major organ give out on me, but it felt like that's what happened. I wasn't sure I was going to be able to survive.

The entire time I was waiting for it to be fixed, I was stressing about what I was missing out on. Was my wife trying to get in touch with me? Was something wrong with our kids? Did my manager have urgent news on a deal we'd been working on? Was Twitter blowing up over some scandal I wouldn't be in the loop about? Had one of my tweets gotten a thousand retweets and I was missing out on the chance to bask in the glory of my accomplishment? All those questions kept racing through my mind.

Of course, when I finally did get my phone back, nothing earth-shattering had happened at all. Yes, I had received some texts and emails, but nothing that had to be handled immediately. Sure, Twitter had blown up over something, but when isn't that happening? There was nothing I needed to chime in on.

In that moment I wondered, why did I feel like stress was eating me alive? Nothing serious happened. I hadn't missed out on shit!

FOMO

Social media is training us to compare our lives, instead of appreciating everything we are. No wonder why everyone is always depressed.
—Bill Murray

Fear of missing out, or FOMO, is what drives so much of our collective social media anxiety. We all think social media is where the party is. Gay, straight, black, white, thugs, theater nerds, sports fans, political fanatics, new parents, grandparents, dog lovers, cat lovers, Republicans, Democrats, Libertarians, it doesn't matter—social media is like one big, popping party that never ends, and everyone is invited. If you're not there, you feel like you are missing out.

Not to mention this forever-lit party doesn't have a bouncer and doesn't charge a cover. Only on social media can some digital dickhead sitting in his underwear in the basement of his mom's house in New Mexico find himself having a conversation with Diddy. Who doesn't want to hang out at a club like that every night? Sure as hell beats whatever's happening in that basement!

But like any party, it's only healthy in small doses. You can't spend your entire day on the digital dance floor. You can't head to the bar for another drink every hour. You can't spend your entire life trying to get into the VIP room.

You have to accept that you're going to miss out on a lot of that party—most of it in fact—if you want to stay functional in the rest of your life. You see what happens to people who party too much in real life? It's no different with the social media party.

Instead of "What am I missing out on?" the question you need to start asking yourself is "How can I refocus on what *is* actually happening in my life?" The answer is like with any addiction, you need to take baby steps one day at a time.

The first step is to think of your phone as a tool, not a part of you. It can be very useful, but you don't need it. When you wake up, the first thing you do shouldn't be pick up your phone to see who texted you while you were asleep. If that's what you do, acknowledge it and then create a different ritual.

When I wake up at four thirty in the morning, after going to pee (with both hands free), I come back to my room and take a few minutes to pray. I make sure to thank God for another day and then ask for divine protection for myself, family, and friends.

Then I take a shower. Next I sit down and read a couple pages from one of my daily-affirmation books. Currently the two I'm using are *The Daily Stoic* by Ryan Holiday and *Your Best Life Begins Each Morning* by Joel Olsteen. After giving my wife and kids a quick kiss goodbye while they sleep, I get in my truck to drive into work.

In the past I used to listen to hip-hop on the way in, but lately I've been riding in silence. I want to use that forty or so minutes to let my brain be still. I may listen to Oprah's *Super-Soul Conversations* podcast or Malcolm Gladwell's *Revisionist History* because I can learn things from those programs. I also listen to sermons by one of my favorite pastors, like John Gray, Carl Lentz, or Steven Furtick. What I won't listen to is anything that's going to plant negative seeds in my mind.

Not until I get to work at 6:00 a.m. do I look at my phone. No texts, no calls, no emails until I walk into that studio. You might say, "Bro, you're still on your phone at six a.m.!" but remember, I've already been up for an hour and a half. When was the last time you waited an hour and a half after you woke up to look at your phone? I bet it's been a while.

I wait because I've come to understand the first move in the morning sets the tone for the rest of the day. It reflects what's most important to you. I simply refuse to put my phone in the same routine as prayer, receiving positive affirmations, and kissing my wife and kids. I might have an issue, but my addiction isn't that strong.

DON'T READ THE COMMENTS

I do struggle with it enough that recently I asked my therapist for advice on how to spend less time on social media. Especially reading comments about myself. Her advice was so simple that I felt stupid for even asking. "Why do you have to be on it?" she asked me.

I mumbled something like, "Easier said than done. Is this what I pay you a hundred and fifty dollars an hour for?" But honestly she was right.

"Why do you have to read the comments on your pages?" she continued. "What is it you're looking for? Do you think someone's going to tell you something about yourself that you don't already know? Of course not. You don't have to read them."

Her last statement really made me think. We've gotten to a point where we feel like Facebook, Twitter, Instagram, Snapchat are *necessary* parts of our lives. It's not true. We make the choice to be on them. Once we do, however, we lose the right to complain about their effect on us.

If you go to the same restaurant over and over but always complain about the food after each meal, ultimately the problem doesn't lie with the restaurant. It lies with your decision-making skills. Yeah, maybe the first time you ate there it was OK, but if you spend the rest of the night on the toilet every time after that, then stop going back!

It's the same with social media. Myspace was cool back in the day. It allowed us to connect with people, hear their music, and keep up with their lives. But it wasn't on our phones. We barely had laptops then, so you had to be on a desktop in your office or at home to even log on. The only time I'd be on Myspace was late at night when I usually wouldn't be interacting with other people anyway. I would go to someone's page, maybe look at pictures, listen to some music, and then keep it moving. I never feared I was missing out on anything that happened there. I checked in when I wanted to, not when I thought I had to.

The shift started after apps like Twitter and Facebook became compatible with phones. At first I resisted joining Twitter, but Lil Duval kept telling me to get on it. I had just got fired from Wendy Williams's radio show and was unemployed, so it was literally something to pass time when I had nothing else to do. Which was more often than I liked.

I would tweet things out, but I didn't know people could reply to them. So for months I was essentially talking to myself until one day I hit that @ reply button and suddenly I saw I had mentions and replies to my tweets. That's when things changed. Suddenly it felt like I had an audience. There was a real sense of call-and-response. It was intoxicating that I could write something and get an immediate reaction. Same thing with Instagram; I could post pictures and people leave comments in real time? I could get an immediate sense of validation? Of acceptance? Of action? That's when it started to feel like I was a part of something bigger than me. The feeling of never having to be alone was addictive.

What we're learning today is that it's important to be alone sometimes. Especially with your thoughts. It's not healthy to go from reading an article about something, to seeing people's tweets about it, to listening to a podcast about it. It's information overload. We need to step back more.

Please realize that it's OK to have downtime with yourself. Creating that time can be something as active as meditating or as passive as commuting in silence. You might feel like you're missing out on something on social media, but what you really might be missing out on are your best ideas. Often our greatest ideas are born in silence. Why do you think a lot of people come up with amazing things while they're taking a shower? Because there's no distractions in there!

In those minutes of silence without your phone, you can reflect. You can get in touch with your thoughts and take stock of what's happening in your life. The key is to extend those minutes of reflection and silence throughout your day. But my god, once they make a phone that you can take in there we really will be addicted to algorithms.

See if you can train yourself to put your phone down when you come home from work and limit yourself to how many times you check it. If setting it on your kitchen table is too tempting, then put it in a drawer or box. Only let yourself check it once before you go to bed. That probably sounds impossible, but if you do it a couple of times you'll find it's not too hard.

Then build on that by undergoing a social media detox. That's right, just like it's important to detox from alcohol or unhealthy foods from time to time, you need to do the same with social media. You can start by going through your phone and deleting one app that you're currently using but isn't essential. You don't have to start with Twitter or Instagram; pick something that you use but in the back of your mind know you don't really need. Then a month later, pick another one. Keep going and building momentum until you're able to delete one of the big ones.

If that feels too hard, you can install an app that limits the time you can spend on social media. When I'm writing, I like an app called Freedom, which blocks all websites and apps. It's like an airport setting for your apps. Or you can try apps like BreakFree or Moments that will allow you to use apps but only for a limited amount of time. It might seem counterintuitive to use an app to break your addiction to apps, but if that's what it takes, don't fight it.

You will likely feel actual withdrawal symptoms. Remember, these apps are designed by computers to keep you hooked. Even crack doesn't have that going for it. Notice that if you stay off some of these apps longer than usual, they'll start sending you reminders. *Hey, check out how many notifications you've missed. Hey, you've got a new friend!* The algorithms can tell you're starting to stray, and the apps will do everything within their power to bring you back. It's like a drug dealer waving a free sample in your face when he hasn't seen you on the block for a minute. It's not going to be as simple as just walking away. You're going to have to fight the urge, often created by the app itself, to jump back on your phone and check in with the bullshit.

It will be hard, but it will be worth it too. Think about how many hours you waste scrolling through hot takes that are really lukewarm and arguments you don't care about. What if you replaced that time with going to the gym? Learning how to cook? Or even just taking a walk. Think about how much better your life would be in a few months.

Even better still, use the time you were spending on social media to be with your family. No amount of likes, no number of retweets, no amount of followers will ever come close to making you happier than spending time with the people you love. Or getting to meet the person you will come to love. If you take one thing from this book, let it be that.

So Anxiousssssss Clinical Correlation by Dr. Ish

The vivid description of Charlamagne's first panic attack goes straight to the core of the intense fear that every person with anxiety or panic has ever felt: they're going to die. In that moment of panic we look for something that's happening simultaneously to blame for this feeling, no matter how illogical it may be, because we're battling for our very survival. Then we try to connect the object of our blame with something from our past that's made us feel a similar way, in order to help the association make sense in our minds . . . even if there isn't a connection. Then our brains spring forward and desperately try to figure out is this problem going to be permanent? Is this going to happen every time I do something like this, and is this feeling going to stay with me and ultimately limit me in life from doing the things I want to do? The real answer to that question is a resounding no. Unfortunately it's hard to reach that conclusion when your mind and body are being riddled with anxiety symptoms that you have no idea how to make go away. Our brains begin to automatically make false connections between what we're thinking and feeling, then our emotions make false associations between what we're feeling and actually doing, and so the pathological pattern begins. Automatic thoughts leading to false assumptions leading to misguided emotions. This creates one of the most common types of anxiety called anticipatory anxiety. We're expecting the worst even though the situation and our symptoms don't indicate it.

Before moving forward, let's be clear on exactly what anxiety means. Everybody worries. Everybody gets nervous. Just because you get anxious sometimes doesn't mean you have an anxiety disorder; of which there are many types. The tool we use as psychiatrists to diagnose anxiety and other mental health disorders is called the *Diagnostic and Statistical Manual of Mental Disorders*, or *DSM-5*, for short.* Here anxiety is defined specifically as "the presence of excessive anxiety and worry about a variety of topics, events, or activities that occurs more often than not for at least six months and is clearly excessive." This means you worry even when there's nothing to worry about, or your worrying is extremely exaggerated in relation to the risk you actually face. You spend a lot of time per day worrying about things and will often seek reassurance from others. You find it difficult to control this worry and are experiencing at least three of the following emotional or physical symptoms:

*Deborah R. Glasofer, "Generalized Anxiety Disorder: Symptoms and Diagnosis," *Verywell Mind*, updated July 3, 2018, verywellmind.com/dsm-5-criteria -for-generalized-anxiety-disorder-1393147.

- Restlessness or feeling on edge
- Tiring easily; more fatigued than usual
- Poor concentration or feeling as though the mind goes blank
- Irritability (which may or may not be observable to others)
- Increased muscle aches or soreness
- Poor sleep (trouble falling asleep or staying asleep, restlessness at night, or sleep that's not restful)
- Sweating, nausea, or diarrhea
- Because of this worry you now find it hard to carry out day-to-day activities and responsibilities and it may spill over and cause problems in your relationships at work or in other important areas.

There is no medical condition that's causing these symptoms (even though there are many medical conditions that can mimic these conditions such as cardiac or gastro-intestinal problems), and the symptoms are not due to the effect of substances, including prescription medication, alcohol, or recreational drugs (e.g., smoking the wrong type of marijuana).

And as any anxiety sufferer will tell you, any one of these symptoms can open the floodgates for all the other symptoms to come rushing through in what can feel like an endless feedback loop that, at its absolute worst, makes you think you're going to die.

The great thing Charlamagne was able to do during his first panic attack is what every good therapist will encourage: trace the problem to its source. What I've learned as a psychiatrist is that the source of most mental problems starts much earlier than when you start to notice symptoms.

A big takeaway from this chapter is understanding the pathway anxiety takes to manifest in our minds. The day we as children realize that we're unique or different can be both the most incredible and most tragic day of our lives. Understanding that "I'm different" and "I'm me" should feel amazing, and it usually does, right up until the moment you realize everyone won't accept you for being you . . . and then it doesn't. And at this stage of mental development in our preadult and often preteen brains, the last thing we want to do is stand out. We want to be a part of the group. We want to be accepted. We want to fit in. Wear the same cool clothes. Listen to the same cool music. Sit at the same cool kids' table. Do the things that cool kids do. And to that end we'll go out of our way to hide the fact that yes, indeed, I'm not like the rest of them. The irony here is that we're all the same in that every single one of us has had this same realization and experienced this sense of longing to belong. The true difference as we grow up is seen in what vehicles, positive or negative, we choose to achieve that belonging. Charlamagne hid in the wooded area of his neighborhood to be alone with his differences, gathered himself, put his mask back on, and rejoined the group. We all wear a mask, then and now. Whether it's in the form of doing things you know you shouldn't in order to fit in, liking people or posts you don't particularly care for because everyone else does, or, worse yet, disliking people simply because everyone else you think you identify with does so too. Think about the things we've surrounded ourselves with since we were kids just to belong: T-Ball, soccer, cheer, dance, sports, fraternities, sororities, neighborhoods, political affiliations; I can say with utmost certainty that at some point you found yourself trying to belong to a group that deep down you knew really didn't suit you. Ninety percent of the decisions we make in life—what to wear, what to eat, what to be, where to live, even who to love—are based on how we imagine our peer group will react. Think about that. When the things you think, feel, and consequently do don't match up with who you are inside, we call that incongruence. It creates internal conflict, and that internal struggle comes out in the most peculiar and sometimes horrific ways. The goal of any good therapist is to help you resolve that internal conflict and become truly comfortable in your own skin without any mask at all; clinically we call that being integrated. Integration goes a long way to resolving your anxiety.

Another of the critical take-home messages here is that in order to grow up to be an emotionally healthy, well-adjusted adult, every child has to have a degree of certainty maintained throughout their childhood. When kids go to bed at night and wake up in the morning, they need to know they're going to be OK. In addition to the day we realize we're different, the other tragic day that can happen in a child's life is the day we realize that certainty is lost. For Charlamagne this came in the form of a natural disaster, but for a lot of kids it can be more generic things. Mom and Dad arguing or fighting. Either parent not being there. Divorce. Death of a close family member. Illness. A household with a high level of emotional expression or a drama-filled family. Just being plain broke and growing up in a financially unstable household. Anything that triggers a kid to think "Everything is not OK" will suffice to inject their first sense of uncertainty in the world and introduce them to their first pang of anxiety.

A child's preadult mind processes the world internally so a child will innately look inward for the answers to the poor questions that his or her child brain is asking to figure out why these things are happening. Why did the storm take our house away? Why did Mom get sick? Why doesn't Dad love me enough to come around? Why don't they love me enough to stay together? Why did Mommy's new friend touch my privates? What did I do wrong to make them go away? What did I do wrong to make this bad thing happen to me? Unfortunately, your brain will look to solve any question you ask it, good, bad, or otherwise, so it's of the utmost importance that you ask yourself only good questions. Ask a poor question and your brain has no choice but to give you an equally poor and useless answer. The answer to all these horrible kid questions of uncertainty leads one inexorably to the damning conclusion: this bad thing happened to me because who I am isn't enough. I'm bad. I'm not good enough. I'm not going to have everything I need in this world to be OK. And then we freak out. Bam. Anxiety.

CHAPTER 3

Blackanoid

"I think anxiety is also something that I'm just now being exposed to. A really big conversation and idea that I'm getting introduced to right now is black mental health. 'Cause for a long time that wasn't a thing that we talked about."
—Chance the Rapper

Anxiety and blackness seems to go hand in hand. It's like African-Americans have permanent PTSD that dates back to slavery.

Post-traumatic stress disorder is a condition usually associated with soldiers who have a difficult time adjusting to civilian life because of the terrible things they've witnessed during war. A vet who might still dive for cover every time a car backfires. Or gets flashbacks of his tank blowing up every time he smells gas when he's filling up his car. Or has vivid dreams about his buddies getting killed every time he goes to sleep.

PTSD is about feeling lingering trauma from a past experience, and from going to therapy and learning more about mental heath, I feel like it has to be a big piece of my anxiety and part of the story of being black in America.

This is how the National Institute of Mental Health defines the condition:

> *PTSD is a disorder that develops in some people who have experienced a shocking, scary, or dangerous event. . . . Nearly everyone will experience a range of reactions after trauma, yet most people recover from initial symptoms naturally. Those who continue to experience problems may be diagnosed with PTSD. People who have PTSD may feel stressed or frightened even when they are not in danger.* *

While PTSD is often associated with soldiers, it is definitely not limited to people who served in wars. There's plenty of traumatic stress experienced by people during their day-to-day lives here in America. Especially black people.

The damage isn't just limited to contemporary events either. The traumatic legacy of slavery is still felt by African-Americans hundreds of years later. I know there are going to be people on the right who hear that and will claim I'm practicing "victimology," or simply tell me and other black folks to "get over it already." To them I would like to say, "Suck my seven-and-a-half-inch dick" (eight inches in the summer). Because inherited trauma is real.

Consider this: a few years ago researchers at New York's Mount Sinai Hospital did a study on a group of Holocaust survivors and their children. The study found that the children of the survivors had stress levels in their genes that couldn't be

---

*"Post-Traumatic Stress Disorder," nimh.nih.gov/health/topics/post-traumatic-stress-disorder-ptsd/index.shtml.

attributed to the relatively healthy and untroubled lives they were living in America. "The gene changes in the children could only be attributed to Holocaust exposure in the parents," said lead researcher Rachel Yehuda. This idea that a parent can pass trauma to a child and subsequent generations is called "epigenetic inheritance." The researchers studied other groups that weren't exposed to extreme stress, but didn't find any other examples of trauma being passed down through genetics.

They must not have studied any black folks then, because there is no question in my mind that just as with those Holocaust survivors, the trauma of slavery has been passed down generation to generation in my family. There's no way that generations of people can be robbed, cheated, humiliated, lied to, and killed without it having a physical impact on their descendants. I hope they do more studies on this phenomenon, but this time testing some decedents of American's systemic racism.

Fight or Flight

One of our most primitive functions is what's known as the "fight-or-flight response." It represents a choice we face each time we enter into what we perceive to be a dangerous situation—should we stick around and fight, or haul ass out of there in flight?

The fight-or-flight response was incredibly useful back in the day when we were out on the savanna hunting for food. Let's say you came upon a gazelle. Your fight-or-flight would process the information and then probably tell your brain to grab a spear and go get your dinner. But if you came around a bend and saw a sleeping lion, it would immediately tell you to break out of there and don't look back, unless you wanted to become dinner yourself.

The fight-or-flight response also changes your body chemistry to make sure you're physically amped up enough to get out of the situation. If you needed to run from a lion, the fight-or-flight response would immediately start pumping stress hormones like adrenaline and cortisol into your bloodstream. Those are the chemicals that allow you to run faster, or fight harder, than you thought you could when you need to survive.

Here's the thing: despite their potentially lifesaving qualities, adrenaline and cortisol are not necessarily healthy for you in the long term. Because of their power, those hormones are also extremely toxic and stay in your body for several days after they're released. You only want them flowing through your blood when it's *absolutely* necessary.

The problem for black folks is that our fight-or-flight sensors have gotten knocked completely out of whack since we were forcibly brought here to America as slaves. Hundreds of years of being slandered, harassed, targeted, and murdered for nothing other than having dark skin has left our fight-or-flight response turned all the way up. We're living in a modern society, yet we constantly find ourselves back on the proverbial savanna. Except now we're the only ones being hunted. We keep pumping all those toxins into our body on a daily basis, even though we don't need them. And it's making us sick. This is how Debra Barksdale, a professor at Virginia Commonwealth University, describes the dangerous effect that toxicity can have on African-Americans:

> *Whether it's related to the pressures from society, increased chances of being stopped by the authorities, trying to pro-*

vide for their families, or trying to find a job or to sustain a job, when a stressor occurs, there are physiological processes that occur in the brain that trigger the release of cortisol. What we have found was in certain people who are constantly stressed, cortisol levels do not go down throughout the day. It will remain high.

When your stress levels are chronically high, it can create all sorts of lasting damage. Physically, it can lead to diabetes, which African-American men are almost twice as likely to develop as white men. It can also dramatically increase your blood pressure, which might explain why, according to the American Heart Association, "the prevalence of high blood pressure in African-Americans is the highest in the world."* No wonder that African-Americans are 1.5 times more likely to die of heart disease than whites.

Chronic stress can also lead to anxiety. There's no question the stress I experienced as an African-American, especially a poor one growing up in the South, has directly led to my issues with anxiety. For a long time I didn't want to admit that, but thankfully now I'm at a place in my life where I can face my anxiety head-on. By understanding where it's rooted, I can also figure out how to get past it. To get better.

Getting better, I should add, naturally. When African-Americans do manage to see a mental health professional with symptoms of PTSD like anxiety, loneliness, and insomnia, it seems like too often we are given some type of medication and

*American Heart Association, "African-Americans and Heart Disease, Stroke," updated August 22, 2017, heart.org/HEARTORG/Conditions/More /MyHeartandStrokeNews/African-Americans-and-Heart-Disease-Stroke_ UCM_444863_Article.jsp#.W0a76S3MzBI.

then sent on our way. While some conditions do require medication, it shouldn't be your first or only choice. As my therapist told me when I first discussed my anxiety, "You don't need medicine. You need someone to talk to." I think that may be true for so many of us.

I believe that being black in America has been a major source of PTSD and anxiety for almost my entire life. From a kid growing up in a trailer on a dirt road in South Carolina to a rich so-called celebrity living in a beautiful home, I've found that people's reaction to my skin color has always led to feelings of unease, confusion, and paranoia.

Feeling in the Air

Like many African-Americans, I've experienced more than my fair share of "shocking, scary, or dangerous events." And most of them have involved the police. Dealing with the police has always been traumatic for me. And it's partially my fault. As a teenager I was selling crack and carrying guns, which practically ensured that my interactions with the cops were going to be stressful.

Knowing that I could be arrested at any moment kept me in a state of constant anxiety. I mean, I was selling crack, while I was on probation no less. If I got caught I was going straight to prison. How could I not be worried?

My method for coping with that fear was to try to never be sober. Alcohol gave me liquid courage, but that wasn't ideal because you can't be on the block drunk as fuck. You have to have your wits about you. All my homies smoked weed, and I tried, but I had zero tolerance for it. I must have been smoking sativa back then too because the paranoia the weed induced was like pouring gasoline on the flames my anxiety was already stoking.

It all came to a head one day when I was around eighteen years old. I had tried to cut way down on smoking because I was on probation for a charge of presenting a firearm. That was my version of being responsible.

On this particular day, however, I got really high right before I punched the clock for my shift at the crack spot. Why, I do not know. As the rest of my crew joked around, I got an overwhelming feeling that the cops were going to show up and bust us. "Yo, I think the police coming today," I told my guys, trying my hardest to sound chill. "Maybe we should shut it down."

"Be quiet, man, you're bugging," my partner Jerrell told me dismissively. "You're just high. Relax, everything's good."

Relax was the last thing I could do. As my crew casually watched for approaching fiends, I was overwhelmed with a sense that the cops were coming any second. When no one was looking, I slipped out the back door and into the woods behind our house, where I quickly buried my dope under a tree near the side of the yard. Then I left and went to my mom's house to cool out. But then at home I was too anxious to sit still, so against my gut I decided to go back to the trap.

When I returned, things felt different. It was as if I was viewing the world through a movie camera. The cars driving down the street appeared to me like they were moving in slow motion. I began to focus on little details I would usually ignore—a bird sitting on a telephone wire, a leaf falling from a tree, or a squirrel bouncing across the lawn. It was like I was in a trance.

I know some of you must be saying to yourself, "Nigga, you

were just high as fuck, that weed must have been laced with something," but I promise you it wasn't that. Everyone else had smoked the same weed as me, but none of my folks were in the same state as I was. None of them were gripped by the same paranoia that had a hold over me. And if they were, they sure weren't acting like me.

As I stood in my stupor, a fiend we knew named PJ pulled up. After we sold him his dope, I noticed he was holding a plastic Easter egg, the kind you would hide jelly beans in when you were a kid. "What's that for?" I asked him. "Ah, just something I keep my dope in," PJ replied. As soon as he said that, two undercover vans came barreling into our driveway. We'd been set up. Jerrell, my cousin Anthony, and I took off running. After getting through the woods, we headed to Jerrell's cousin's house and laid low there. I knew the cops weren't chasing me anymore, but even after I stopped and sat under a tree, I still couldn't calm down. All I could think about was how close I'd come to violating my probation. How close I'd been to going back to jail. Of incurring my father's wrath again. Of making my mother cry again.

We stayed at Jerrell's cousin's house for a couple of hours, until I was finally able to breathe normally. It wasn't that I was physically exhausted. I was emotionally broke down. All the paranoia that came with selling crack had finally caught up to me. The constant fear of getting arrested. The never-ending worry that someone from your own crew might be underselling you. Or stealing your money on the low. Or even worse, that another dealer was going to rob you for your dope. And maybe even kill you in the process.

Unfortunately, I never realized just how damaged I'd become. Instead, like so many young African-American men caught up on the street, I thought how I was feeling was "normal." Part of "the game." Being paranoid, we actually used to think, was something positive. We took it as a sign that we were being "on point." Or as Jay-Z would say, "When the streets is watching blocks keep clocking, waiting for you to break, make your first mistake."

Looking back on it, many of the songs from that era we considered "hustler anthems" were really textbook examples of people with undiagnosed anxiety crying out for help. I'm talking about Jay-Z's "Streets Is Watching," Beanie Sigel's "Feel It in the Air," or Geto Boys' "Mind Playing Tricks on Me." Go back and listen to them, you'll see that they were all about anxiety!

Clearly I wasn't alone. Even though I thought I was.

To Protect and Make Paranoid

The anxiety I suffered related to selling drugs might have been self-inflicted, but the paranoia I've experienced in my encounters with police as an adult hasn't been. I've gone out of my way to make my dealings with police as infrequent as possible. When they do occur, I couldn't be more respectful and mindful of following their instructions. Yet every single interaction still fills my heart with dread and makes me shook.

If you're not black, when you see a cop in your rearview mirror, you probably do a quick mental checklist. Am I driving over the speed limit? Did I make an illegal turn? Do I have weed on me? Have I been drinking? Are any of my taillights out? If the answers to those questions are no, then you probably exhale and wait for the cop to pass you.

When you're black, even if the answers are no, you'll still be breathing heavy and gripping the wheel. When a cop pulls up behind me, I immediately become extremely agitated. My mind starts flashing to every story about a routine traffic stop that ended with a black person dead. The thought of those images make me nervous as hell, which in turn makes me feel like I'm doing something wrong. I start to question all my actions: Am I going too slow, or should I try to stay exactly at the speed limit? Should I turn my music down, or will a cop see my hand move and think I'm trying to hide something? Should I get my license and registration out now, put them on the dashboard, so when he comes I can already have my hands hanging out the window? Or if I open my glove compartment, will he think I'm going for a gun? And then kill me?

Those questions race through my mind so fast that I start to feel like I can't drive straight. I'll pull into the first gas station or strip mall I see, just so I can get off the road and calm down. And that's without the cop ever once flashing his lights at me.

God forbid a cop actually does put on his blue lights and pull me over. It happened one morning recently when a cop pulled me over as I was coming out of the Holland Tunnel into New Jersey. Through my rearview mirror, I watched two cops get out of the car, one walking up to the driver's side, the other to the passenger side. They walked slowly, hands on hips, turning the tension up even higher. "Damn," I thought as they approached. "Getting taken out by a cop can really happen this fast."

When one cop got to the driver's window, I already had both hands on the steering wheel. He asked for my license and registration and I replied, "Is it OK if I reach for it?" He could hear the "I don't want you to kill me for no damn reason" tone in my voice, so he said, "Sure," and then took my license. He went back to his car and ran it. I don't know how long it actually takes for police to run a license, but it seems to me like they like to milk the moment for all it's worth. They probably get the data in thirty seconds, but then they like to sit there and let you sweat a few more minutes just to remind you who is boss. For African-Americans, this reminder is always a little more affecting. When a cop keeps you waiting in your car, the unsaid message seems to be, "You ain't moving until we decide you're going to move. Slavery might be over, but you're not really free unless we say you are." That's a very chilling message to receive.

In this case, the cops let me stew for a few minutes and then brought my license back. "Make sure you don't drive too fast coming out the tunnel," the cop told me evenly and then let me go. That was it. No ticket. No more drama.

I should have been mad, because I know for a fact I wasn't speeding. The cops were just running licenses in the hopes that they could catch someone with a warrant or expired plates. I should have complained for getting pulled over for no reason, but instead I actually told the cop, "Thank you, sir, I appreciate it." I was just happy I didn't get shot! For the rest of the ride, I had that anxious feeling in my chest similar to how I used to feel back in Moncks Corner. The feeling that I had narrowly escaped a brush with a force looking to do me harm.

I hate to admit it, but getting shot during a traffic stop is always in the back of my mind when I'm driving. It's PTSD from all we are living through. I feel like I'm stuck in this trauma partially because of the videos we see of unarmed black men and women getting murdered on TV. On one hand, I'm thankful the rest of the world is finally getting visual proof of what African-Americans have always maintained: cops often shoot black people for no good reason. I have to believe that over time these images will make all the nonbelievers and skeptics out there get behind movements like Black Lives Matter and force the powers that be to make some real reform when it comes to how cops interact with African-Americans.

It's especially difficult when my wife and my kids are with me. Suppose we get pulled over and a nervous officer mistakes my daughter's phone for a gun and shoots her? Suppose a cop pulls my wife out of her car Sandra Bland–style and ends up killing her? The idea that a police officer could hurt them—with me present—freaks me out. If that was to happen I know without a shadow of a doubt I am going to die in that moment because I'm not going to stand by and watch some cracker-ass cracka racist cop physically assault my family. God forbid I'm ever in this situation.

I'll try to switch my thoughts up when I feel myself dwelling on that possibility, but I find it very difficult to shut those scenarios out of my mind. To make matters worse, I start beating myself up for *not* being able to get out of my own head. "Damn, man, you're weak," I'll tell myself. "You're letting these devils get the best of you. Man the fuck up!" Such is the irony of being black in America. You end up getting mad at yourself for not being better at dealing with the possibility that a government employee might kill you for no reason. These cops might not even be giving me a second thought, but I'm twisting myself in all sorts of emotional knots based on the possibility that they *might*.

Whenever a new video comes out of a cop killing an African-American I try not to watch it, but I still feel myself drawn to it. Again, I don't think white people understand how devastating these images are. When you see people who look like you killed over and over again for no reason other than *they look like you*, it's impossible not to start thinking, "One day I might be next." That's not paranoia; it's actually a very logical way to see things.

I hate to make the analogy, but imagine if every time someone shot up a country musical festival in Las Vegas, or a movie theater in Colorado, we actually saw those murders on TV. The same way I saw Eric Garner getting choked out by cops on Staten Island, or Walter Scott getting gunned down in South Carolina. That would be incredibly stressful and traumatic for a large part of the population.

We don't see those images though. We aren't shown white children, or even white adults, getting shot on TV. It's considered too disturbing—for good reason. But when an African-American gets shot, we're going to witness it. Over and over again. I pray those images lead to real change. But in the meantime, they're creating real damage. That's pretty much the definition of PTSD. Reliving traumatic events like they just happened. Finding yourself trapped by your fears, day after day, year after year, even if they're no longer an immediate threat.

Questioning Myself

While cops make me instantly anxious, I've been fortunate to avoid blatant racism—unlike too many African-Americans. I haven't been hit by its hardest blows. I'm pretty sure I have dealt with more covert racism than overt. The Klan never burned a cross on the lawn in front of our trailer. Or made my daddy disappear for not "knowing his place." Just as no white man ever threatened me for talking to a white woman, or called me a nigger (at least to my face).

But growing up in South Carolina, I definitely felt that kind of energy in the air. Like a fog that never quite lifted. I first sensed it, even if I couldn't name it, back in elementary school. One of my teachers, let's call her "Ms. Suspected White Supremacist," was definitely a racist. At the time I thought she was just mean, but now I can see she really had it out for her black students. There was a black kid in our class named Alferd Copen who was really poor. None of us were rich, but Alferd's family seemed to be doing even worse than everyone else's. His clothes looked like rags, he had holes in his sneakers, and he would sometimes smell. He also seemed to be hungry most of the time. At lunchtime he would wolf down his school lunch and then go around trying to snatch up other people's leftovers, probably so he could take them home and eat them for dinner. Usually a kid like that will get made fun of, but his situation was so bad that we'd actually go out of our way to give him some of our lunches.

That empathy didn't extend to Ms. Suspected White Supremacist. Rather than cut the poor kid a break, she would be unusually tough on him. Worst of all, if he messed up in class, Ms. Suspected White Supremacist would refuse to let him go down to the cafeteria for lunch, as a punishment. I watched this poor little boy cry painful tears whenever that would happen.

Wasn't just black kids either. There was another little girl in our class named Maria Serano, who I believe was Mexican. Maria was a good kid, minded her business, but one day Ms. Suspected White Supremist didn't like something she did and literally picked this little girl up and tossed her around the classroom. Maria was crying her eyes out, but the rest of us just put our heads down on our desks and stayed quiet because Ms. Suspected White Supremacist had conditioned us not to cross her.

Ms. Suspected White Supremacist even came at me because I was a Jehovah's Witness and couldn't celebrate holidays or pledge allegiance to the flag. Once during Christmas she had the class work on making lists of what sorts of presents they wanted. Since that didn't apply to me, she gave me some math assignments to stay busy with. I was sitting at my desk, working on them quietly, when suddenly Ms. Suspected White Supremacist announced to the whole class, "Lenard, just because you don't like Christmas doesn't mean you have to ruin it for everyone else!"

What? I hadn't said a word to anyone! Obviously I didn't personally have anything against Christmas. If anything, I was *jealous* of my classmates who were talking about the G. I. Joes, Nintendos, and new sneakers they were going to get. Ms. Suspected White Supremacist said that because she wanted to humiliate me.

My crime wasn't being a Jehovah's Witness. It was having black skin. I'm confident in saying that because for all the physical abuse she did with the black and brown kids, I never saw her speak harshly to one of the white kids. Let alone deny them food, or put her hands on them. Never.

But this is all in hindsight. When you're in fourth grade, you don't question these things. You believe the people in power know what they're doing. If anything, you begin to question yourself. "*Did* I say something bad about Christmas?" you wonder. "Was Maria sassy with the teacher and deserve what she got?" It doesn't even occur to you that this adult, in a position of power no less, might actually hate you because of something so illogical as the color of your skin.

As I got older, the racism around me came into much clearer focus. If I was driving with my father and someone passed us in a pickup with a Confederate flag (which was often), my father would state, "Look at those cracka-ass crackers." (My father was never one for subtlety.) I would immediately register, "OK, those white people are racist."

For better or for worse, in South Carolina racism was pretty cut-and-dried. Racist white folks weren't going to any great lengths to conceal how they felt about us. To give you an example, one of the most popular barbecue restaurants in the state was a joint in Columbia called Maurice's Piggie Park. It was owned by a man named Maurice Bessinger, who was a stone-cold racist. I'm talking the type of racist who, if you aren't from the South, you probably aren't used to encountering. Forget about the huge Confederate flag he had waving in the parking lot; back in the sixties he went to the state supreme court to argue that he shouldn't have to serve black customers. When that didn't work, Maurice would sell pamphlets at his restaurant explaining why slavery and segregation were actually good things (he'd even give patrons a discount if they bought one).

Did this overtly racist attitude run Maurice out of business? Did it make him a pariah to the good people of South Carolina? Hell no. White folks would flock to the Piggie Park for some collards and pulled pork, or a beef brisket sandwich. Maurice was so popular that in the nineties he began selling frozen barbecue and hot sauce nationally. At one point he had the largest commercial barbecue operation in the *entire country*.

When I got older and moved to Columbia, seeing Maurice being so successful used to really get under my skin. Not only did I refuse to eat there myself, but I used to have fantasies of blowing the Piggie Park up with a bazooka. I would do it the exact same way one of Saint Louis's boys used a rocket to blow up Dollar Bill's spot in *The Players Club*. (If you don't know what I'm talking about, shame on you for never experiencing the cinematic magic that is *The Players Club*.)

Overt or Covert

Growing up in this environment in the South I just came to assume that most white people were racist until proven otherwise.

That might seem like a depressing way to move through life, but it actually didn't stress me out that much. I liked that in the South, you generally can sense where people stand on race. There's not a lot of ambiguity.

For instance, there is a restaurant called the Barony House in Moncks Corner that I had never eaten in. I'd drive by it all the time, but for whatever reason I never went in. One time my wife (who was my girlfriend then) and I decided to give it a try. The moment we walked through the doors, we were blinded by all the light. By that, I mean we could see that the patrons and the staff were completely white.

When the hostess came over to seat us, we both hesitated. Finally I said, "Actually, I think we're going to pass. We don't need menus."

She just looked at us and then said, verbatim, "Why, too many white people?"

"Exactly," we both said.

"I understand," she replied evenly.

Now, if that same scenario had played out in New York or New Jersey, it would have probably turned into a big scene. If a hostess had sensed that we didn't want to be seated because there were too many white people in a restaurant, she would have probably bent over backward protesting that the place wasn't racist, that there was nothing to worry about. And she might have been sincere. But in my mind, when you walk into a space and see you are outnumbered seventy-five to two, then it's best to keep things moving. Otherwise, you are just setting yourself up for a random act of racism. Why put yourself in that position?

Another time, I was down in West Virginia with my friend the comedian Lil Duval to film a special for MTV called *From the Mud to Manhattan*. It featured us visiting some of the stars of the MTV show *Buckwild*, which was basically the hillbilly version of *Jersey Shore*, in their home state. One of the stars of *Buckwild* was my late, great friend Shain Gandee. He was an incredible spirit, unlike anyone I'd ever met before. On the surface he looked just like one of the white boys I'd grown up seeing around Moncks Corner: he drove a pickup truck with a Confederate flag on the back and squirrel tails hanging from the antenna. He'd wear camouflage T-shirts and hunting caps and had a wispy mustache. But he was different from those guys I'd seen growing up. He had heart. A unique view of life, which he was committed to living to the absolute fullest. He didn't own a cell phone. He called them "space boxes" and said he'd rather be free than a slave to a box. He was just a kid, twenty-one years old, but he already understood the value of living for the moment and not getting caught up in distractions. I've always remembered that.

One day during filming we were driving around on a freezing winter day. I'm a country boy myself, so it was nothing for me to dress like Shain and his friends: full camouflage hunting suit, big camp jacket, and a ski mask. At one point we pulled into a drugstore to get something, and I bounded out of the car with my ski mask pulled over my face. Shain put his arm out and stopped me in my tracks before saying, "Charlamagne, don't go in there with that ski mask, you're a *nigga* in West Virginia. They will shoot you dead."

That was probably the first time a white person referred to me as nigga, directly to my face, but I couldn't even be mad. The anxiousness in Shain's voice was unmistakable, and I could tell he was genuinely afraid for me. He knew the sight of a black man wearing a ski mask, even if he was in town filming a TV special, would put fear in the hearts of those white devils. Fear that they might very well act on. I appreciated his warning, even if he had to use that word to get his point all the way across. (Sadly, Shain died a few months later from carbon monoxide poisoning when the SUV he was driving became partially submerged in some deep mud he and his friend and uncle were driving around in for sport. As much as we went "mudding" when we were together in West Virginia, I don't think he would have wanted to go out any other way.)

While I obviously don't want to get shot by a trigger-happy West Virginia cracker, those sorts of overtly racist white people have never bothered me too much. If I encounter some tiki torch–carrying white boys in beige slacks and white polo shirts, that's easy for me to deal with. I'll just say, "Fuck you," and keep it moving. Someone being openly racist toward me isn't my problem; it's *their* problem. Something is wrong with them for being racist. Nothing is wrong with me for being the victim of their racism.

Overt racism doesn't slow me down or give me anxiety at all. It's the subtle, passive-aggressive, "not sure if it's there" racism that gets me stuck in my own head.

Racial Profiling

Once I started making money, one of the first things I did was move into a "nice" area of Teaneck, New Jersey. What makes it "nice"? Well, the houses are big. The lawns are manicured. Schools are good. But probably the area's biggest selling point was that there weren't any "niggers" living in it. Except for me.

That's not exactly true, there was plenty of "niggatry" in my new neighborhood, it was just coming from my white neighbors. I'll give you an example. One afternoon a few years back I was in my house getting ready for the premiere of Mona Scott-Young's *The Gossip Game*, which featured my *Breakfast Club* cohost Angela Yee. Around 5:00 p.m. my good friend Wax pulled up in front of my home to pick me up. If you read *Black Privilege*, or have listened to my podcast *The Brilliant Idiots*, then you already know Wax is six four, goes about two hundred and sixty pounds, is almost as dark as Akon, and has a head full of dreads.

Wax was a couple of minutes early, so he texted me and said he was going to stay out in front and put on his new tags and license plate he'd just gotten in the mail for his Mercedes.

"No problem," I texted him, and went back to getting ready.

Five minutes later I got another text from Wax reading, "The boys out here"—"boys" being Wax's code for cops.

"What for?" I replied. He didn't answer, so I went outside to investigate.

As soon as I stepped out my door, I saw that two cops had Wax and my boy Shad (who had just pulled up himself) in handcuffs. When one of the cops saw me coming out of my house, he said, "Do you live here with your parents?" That really threw me for a loop because I was over thirty at that point. Why would he ask me that?

"No," I replied. "I live here with my wife and kids, and this is my house. And those are my friends who I invited over. Why are they in handcuffs?"

The cop explained that a neighbor had called to report a suspicious man in front of their house.

"Why is he suspicious?" I asked. "Because he's a black man in front of his black friend's house putting tags on his car in broad daylight?"

"Listen, we're just responding to the call," replied the cop.

"Then why are they both in cuffs?" I asked.

He replied, "Well, we ran their licenses, and they both have unpaid parking tickets."

At that moment my next-door neighbor came running out of his house and started shouting, "I knew it, I knew it! What did they have? Guns? Drugs?"

"No," said the cop. "Just unpaid parking tickets."

The triumphant look on my neighbor's face instantly evaporated. Without another word, he turned around and went back into his house.

The cops eventually let Wax and Shad go, but the whole deal left me extremely uneasy about living in that neighborhood.

From that day on, whenever I saw my neighbor—which was often, as we lived next door to each other—I refused to speak to him. You might say, "Damn right, don't speak to that racist!" but it's not that easy when you're living in the situation instead of reading about it in a book. Our daughters played together all the time. Our wives were friends. It was stressful to have to see him, but I felt like I couldn't tell him what a racist piece of shit he was because I didn't want to create too many waves in our "nice" neighborhood. The stress of getting the silent treatment must have gotten to him, because he did finally come over and apologize to me for his "mistake." We were eventually able to build some common ground over radio. My neighbor's favorite personality was Q104.3's legendary morning man Jim Kerr, who I speak to every day. Off of that we were able to forge a peace, really for the sake of my family. But I never forgot what he did.

A year later, after getting a new radio contract and one too many mixtapes in my mailbox, my wife and I decided to move to a new "nice" neighborhood. Once again, we had no reason to believe that our new neighbors would be closeted racists. We were moving to a more "upscale" area than Teaneck, which up until that point had easily been the most expensive place I'd ever lived in. We were in a thoroughly professional neighborhood, surrounded by doctors, lawyers, and high-paid executives. Less than an hour outside of Manhattan. I shouldn't have any problems there, right?

I found myself starting to get anxious the first October after we moved in. I noticed Halloween decorations popping up on our cul-de-sac that seemed almost devilish in their energy. Granted, that was probably some of my Witness bias (maybe Ms. Suspected White Supremist was right about one thing) seeping through. So I let it go. Hey, there's nothing racist about

Halloween decorations, right? But my suspicions were confirmed as the election grew closer and suddenly "Trump for President" signs started popping up on our street like mushrooms in a cow pasture.

"I knew it!" I exclaimed to myself one day driving through our hood. "These white people are dangerous!" No one had said a word to me, or called the cops on my friends, or hustled their kids inside when I walked by, but I could feel the energy of the neighborhood change. I got so paranoid that I started making my daughter play in our backyard, instead of in front of the house. She used to be able to ride her bike all around our neighborhood, now she's gotta be in our cul-de-sac. I didn't want any racist neighbors to see her and get any bright white ideas.

Some of you might say, "Stop overreacting," but I promise you as a black man it's very unsettling to see Trump signs on your neighbors' lawns. Especially when since 1992 New Jersey has voted Democrat in every presidential election. You are making a statement when you put that sign up, and sorry, it's not "Time for some change in government." Nope, you are saying loud and clear, "Let's make sure America is for whites first and foremost!" And when they look around their "nice" neighborhood, there's only one house ruining their vision for a Pink Person's Paradise: mine. So you're damn right my daughter is only playing in the back!

As a result, even though I paid a lot of money for my five-thousand-square-foot home, I'm never completely comfortable there. I pay my taxes, mow my lawn, don't play music loud, and even make sure Wax parks in my driveway when he comes over. But I still don't feel welcome in my "nice" surroundings. These "well-to-do" white people have me shook.

Boy Is a White Racist Word . . .

I feel equally uneasy during many of my dealings in the entertainment industry. Again, it's a space where I should feel at home. Feel comfortable in my skin and secure in my accomplishments. After all, the perception is that the entertainment industry is one of the most liberal establishments in the country. Media execs and stars give millions of dollars to Democrats every year. They're some of the most outspoken voices against Trump and for diversity. I should be able to relax around these folks, right?

Nope.

One time I was meeting with the president of a *major* television network. I'm talking the three-letter variety, top of the food chain. Toward the end of our meeting he ran down all the different projects I was working on and then exclaimed, "Boy, you are really doing it!" I was stunned. Things started moving in slow motion. He was still talking, but everything sounded muffled. "Did this guy really just call me a boy?" I asked myself. "Did this white man in a suit just insult me and all my ancestors by calling me a boy? What would the 'militant midget' Michael Evans from *Good Times* do?"

I was stunned, but I didn't confront the executive because I didn't know if it was me or him who was bugging. A major executive wouldn't just call a black entertainer "boy" to his face? Or would he?

I had no idea.

As he walked me to the elevator, he stopped to make some small talk with a woman on her way outside. "Boy, it's really cold today," he lightheartedly warned her. When I heard that, I snapped out of my daze. He wasn't a racist, he was just an

old-fashioned dude who peppered his conversation with collo-
quialisms like "boy." He probably said things like "shucks," and
"yes, ma'am" too.

Most people probably wouldn't have even detected a *hint* of
racism in his use of "boy." We were in his office surrounded
by agents, managers, and other executives. Plus he used it in
the middle of telling me how successful, talented, and hardworking I was. Here I was, on the cusp of realizing one of my
dreams, which was to do business with a major TV network.
But instead of being locked in on the business at hand, I found
myself obsessing over whether this man standing in front of me
in a beautifully tailored suit was the type to change into a white
robe and hood when he got home. Why would I do that?

If you've ever struggled with anxiety, you already know how
hard it can be to handle big moments in your career. You're
overthinking every meeting and conversation. You're worrying about if you're outfit is right or if the person you're meeting
with is really familiar with your work. You've got way too much
going through your head. Now with all that going on, imagine
piling on a fear that the guy at the head of the table is actually
a racist.

That's what happened to me. I'd been triggered by the word
even though a white man had never called me "boy" before;
hearing it had sent me somewhere else. Instead of being in a
skyscraper in Manhattan, I was right back in the South with
crackers riding by me in pickups waving the Confederate flag.

Thankfully I didn't act on being triggered. Imagine if I had
cut him off in the middle of his compliment and asked, "Who
the *fuck* are you calling boy?" That probably would have been
one of the most awkward silences of all time, followed by a
lot of nervous laughter from the other people in the room

who would have had no idea why I was tripping. The executive would have apologized, even though he didn't do anything wrong, and acted like everything was all right. But you can best believe I wouldn't be doing any business in the future with that network.

It sounds almost comical when I tell that story now, but my reaction was very real. I've been tossed around on the waves of subtle racism for so long that I have a hard time telling what's up or what's down anymore.

I also have a difficult time discerning whether other people of color have truly been victims of racism or not. An inability that has gotten me in hot water from time to time. A great example is when Amara La Negra, a beautiful Dominican entertainer, came on *The Breakfast Club* to promote her appearance on *Love & Hip Hop*. During her interview, Amara spoke on the colorism darker-skinned Afro-Latinos like herself face. She explained that her darker skin has prevented her from achieving the level of success that lighter-skinned Afro-Latina performers like Cardi B have enjoyed. Even though I know both racism and colorism are real issues, I still had to ask her, "Are you sure it's not all in your head?"

"It's true!" Amara responded, and then proceeded to list all the soap operas, movies, and magazines she felt she had been overlooked by because of her skin. "Everyone's talking about it," Amara said, referring to how her storyline on *Love & Hip Hop* addresses colorism. "And I'm grateful that we are. Because I think we need to discuss certain things and give opportunities to people who look like myself based off their talent and their knowledge and not the way they look."

As soon as the interview hit, social media immediately jumped all over me and accused me of gaslighting her comments:

Charlamagne's aversion to comprehending the struggles of black women in the industry is incredibly clear

Charlamagne tha God is the ultimate anti black fake woke negro for saying colorism doesn't exist in America. (He's 5 shades lighter from when his career started)

You are some true uncle toms. You don't believe racism and colorism exists? Charlamagne always attacks women. Are you gay?

Some of the criticism might have been a little extreme (questioning someone's experience with colorism makes me gay?), but overall it was fair. I *had* made it sound like I was dismissing her experiences.

Part of the problem was we were having two different conversations at the same time: she was talking about colorism in the Latino market and society and I was talking about colorism in the American entertainment business. While she detailed the struggles she faced, I was thinking about the incredible success dark-skin entertainers like Lupita Nyong'o, Viola Davis, SZA, Issa Rae, and Danai Gurira have been experiencing in America lately.

But obviously I should have given her grievances more credibility. I was challenging what she'd gone through and one thing I'm learning is you can't challenge someone's life experiences. If that's what she's dealt with, then my job is to listen. Plus, by my own admission, I don't know much about the Latino market.

I should have just accepted her observations and given her support. The trouble is, as a black man in this entertainment business I never can tell what's real and what's imagined. I was guilty of projecting some of my uncertainty onto her experience.

I had a similar situation when the singer Tory Lanez came on *The Breakfast Club* to talk about a video of him in a high-end clothing store in Vancouver that went viral. He had come to the store with a budget to shop for the wardrobe for a video he was about to shoot. Tory approached a salesperson about helping him but decided the guy was giving him a racist energy. Rather than just leave the store, Tory decided to film himself spending his entire $35,000 budget with another salesperson, while taunting the salesperson he thought was racist.

When I saw the video, it rubbed me the wrong way. I'm not the highest grade of weed in the dispensary, but if an employee of a store is being racist toward me, then that whole store is going to suffer. Not just one employee. Plus, Tory was a little vague on just what the salesperson had done to reveal themselves as racist. So you know where I went. "They're going to hate me for asking this," I said. "But are you sure it wasn't just in your head?"

Tory was adamant about what had happened. "It's a certain look, it's a certain body language," he explained. But then the more we talked about it, he conceded maybe the salesperson's attitude had more to do with the fact that Tory (by his own admission) was dressed kinda bummy. "It might not even have been a race thing. It could have been the way I was dressed," Tory shrugged. "If I want to go shop, I don't want to wear a bunch of tight clothes. I want to be comfortable. . . . Some people come to the store [dressed bummy] like that and waste people's time."

By the end of the conversation, neither of us knew how to accurately interpret the situation. Was the salesperson truly acting racist toward him? Or had Tory misinterpreted the salesperson's energy? Neither of us could tell for sure. Tory even made it clear that he planned to shop at the store in the future.

That's a little insight into how off-balance America (and Canada too, apparently) is. We decide a salesperson is being racist and create a viral moment on social media to expose him, but later on still have no idea if it was real or imagined.

These are the types of anxieties and microaggressions white people *never* have to deal with. If you're white and somebody looks at you funny, it's probably because you didn't shower that morning and look like a mess. Not because they think the very color of your skin looks disgusting! For black folks, we never know for sure. We're always wondering.

The strategy I've developed to deal with people who are offended by my skin color is simple: I refuse to turn down my blackness. If my blackness makes you uncomfortable, then you need to check *your* temperature. I'm not adjusting *my* thermostat because you've got an unnecessary problem.

If anything, I believe white people should be going out of their way to make African-Americans know where they stand on race. A truly conscious white person—an "ally," as woke Twitter might say—will be aware of the sins of their ancestors and try to make up for it by making black people feel more comfortable. By letting their words, actions, and energy let black people know, "Hey, I'm not one of those crackas. No need to get anxious about what I might be thinking."

In *Black Privilege*, I suggested that these allies put their black coworkers at ease by simply going up to them and saying, "Hi, I'm Tanner, and I'm not a white devil!" A lot of readers thought I was joking, but I wasn't. Personally, I would feel much more comfortable around a white coworker if they said that to me. I do admit it is an extreme approach, but extreme problems require extreme solutions.

There are other ways to get the point across that aren't quite so over-the-top. You could start by simply treating your black coworkers the way you would like to be treated. Just treat people like genuine human beings and you will be fine. Don't just run up on me asking have I seen *Black Panther*; don't try to be down and say "Wakanda Forever"; don't tell me that you love the TV show *Atlanta* too! I don't want you to love our culture; I want you to love us. There's a difference.

PTSD and Therapy

Even if all white people get woke, I still believe black people will be dealing with their own PTSD. When I think about that time running from the cops through the woods, or getting pulled over for no reason, I start to get just as anxious as I was when those incidents happened. I can be sitting in my beautiful home in New Jersey, but emotionally I still feel like a teenager who can't breathe and is living in fear.

PTSD is one of the main reasons I'm in therapy today. If I can't deal with my old anxieties, then it's going to be impossible to deal with whatever new issues I encounter in my life.

If you sold drugs and were always running from the cops as a kid, you might suffer from PTSD. If one of your parents got locked up, you might suffer from PTSD. If you were locked up in a jail cell *with* a parent like I was, you probably suffer from PTSD. If you got put in the foster care system, you might suffer from PTSD. If you were sexually abused, you might suffer from PTSD. If one of your parents, a close family member, or a friend was killed, you probably suffer from PTSD. If you've been shot or had a gun pulled on you, you probably suffer from PTSD.

Even if you've "only" experienced racism throughout your

life, you might still be suffering from PTSD. Over time the effects of racism have a corrosive effect on us. It wears away at our emotions until we're overwhelmed by our anxiety and fear. According to Dr. Monnica Williams, a professor at the University of Connecticut, fear of police is a leading cause of undiagnosed PTSD in African-Americans.

> There's a heightened sense of fear and anxiety when you feel like you can't trust the people who've been put in charge to keep you safe. Instead, you see them killing people who look like you. Combined with the everyday instances of racism, like microaggressions and discrimination, that contributes to a sense of alienation and isolation. It's race-based trauma.

So many of us deal with this kind of fear on a daily basis. So many of us experience these microaggressions and face discrimination in our work, personal lives, and social situations.

It has to have a huge impact on our community, but very few of us talk about it. According to a study for the *Journal of Anxiety Disorders*, African-Americans have a 9.1 percent prevalence rate for PTSD (compared to 6.8 percent in whites). In other words, *almost one in ten black people are suffering from PTSD.*

Are you one of them?

One in ten. That's a very high number, but chances are it should be even higher. A lot of African-Americans with PTSD are misdiagnosed with other mental health disorders, especially schizophrenia. Studies have found that many mental health professionals don't believe that African-Americans are intelligent enough to suffer from PTSD. "We did testing and many people didn't see PTSD as a black person's disease because of racist notions," Dr. William Lawson, a former professor of psychiatry at Howard University and a current dean at the University of Texas at Austin, told the *Root*. "PTSD assumes that a person has insight and sensitivity. People assume that black people are invulnerable, that we do not have a functional apparatus to experience any kind of mood complexity."* Ain't that some bullshit?

This is a great example of why systemic racism is so insidious. We're subjected to traumatic experiences almost our entire lives, but when we demonstrate the symptoms of PTSD, we're told it's all in our heads. Or that we're not smart enough to have an emotional reaction to the abuses we suffer. It's no wonder so many of us spend our lives getting high.

PTSD and Me

Self-medication, I can tell you, is not the answer. If you've suffered trauma, there's not enough weed in the world to make it go away. Just like there's not enough booze. Or pills. Or even sex. We try to drown out our pain through those escapes, but they're still sitting there waiting for us whenever we get back.

Some people are going to get mad at me for saying this, but there also aren't enough prayers to fix your trauma. I'll get into this more in the next chapter, but too often in the African-American community we rely on the church to fix our mental health issues. We think the best tonic for some "nerves" is to

*Ericka Blount Danois, "He Cries Alone: Black Men and PTSD," *The Root*, May 24, 2015, theroot.com/he-cries-alone-black-men-and-ptsd-1790859948.

spend Sunday morning in a pew singing and praying. Getting closer to God. The church might be a great place for you to find spiritual growth and fellowship, but it's probably not the right place for you to go for mental health disorders like anxiety and PTSD. For those, you should really talk to a therapist.

One of my favorite scriptures in the Bible is Isaiah 54:17 which starts off, "No weapon formed against you shall prosper." We usually reference that when someone is attacking us, but what about when the things we have *experienced* in life are attacking us? What happens when the trauma you still carry with you turns on you? That's more dangerous than any thief, mugger, or hater.

You better go see a therapist to help you make sure those weapons inside of you don't prosper. But that can be a challenge, since for many African-Americans, therapy is the last place they want to turn. "There is a stigma associated with going to get help," Ron Armstead, the executive director of the Congressional Black Caucus Veterans Braintrust, told the *Root.** "Brothers won't go in to a doctor until they see some blood."

I know that's true, because I felt that way for a long time, but now my therapist is helping me through a technique called cognitive behavioral therapy, or CBT. This could be a good treatment to help you if you find yourself reliving trauma from your past, but there are many other types of therapy too that I'll get into in the next chapter. I'll also get into how I got past my own perceptions of therapy and who I thought it was for (white people).

I'd also highly recommend you consider changing your diet if there's even a chance you might suffer from PTSD. As I men-

* Danois, "He Cries Alone."

tioned, the stress that comes from racism absolutely makes your body create hormones like adrenaline and cortisol. According to the Mayo Clinic, over time the presence of those hormones in your system can lead to such conditions as:

- Anxiety
- Depression
- Digestive problems
- Headaches
- Heart disease
- Sleep problems
- Weight gain
- Memory and concentration impairment

That's pretty much a laundry list of issues a lot of black folks deal with. The good news is that you can fight off a lot of those ailments with a diet that boosts your immunity. The key is avoiding processed food and increasing your intake of "whole" foods. If you're not sure what that means, the easiest way to think of it is anything that comes premade, especially in a bag or can, is processed. If you can't grow it or catch it, it's processed. So potato chips are processed, but a baked potato is a whole food (just keep the cheese off it). A cookie or piece of cake for dessert is processed, but apples or blueberries are whole foods. Pasta is processed, but a salmon filet is a whole food. They're not foods, but think of soda as processed, water as whole.

Even simpler still, eat as many green veggies as possible. I started doing that a few years ago after consulting with my dermatologist, Dr. Natasha Sandy. The initial goal was to help get rid of the dark spots under my eyes, which Dr. Sandy correctly identified as being related to my crappy diet. It was high in processed foods and creating too much inflammation in my body. But as I began to eat more veggies and less junk, an incredible thing started to happen. Not only did the splotches go away, but I started to feel *much* better too (not to mention losing over twenty-five pounds). Not just more energy (which is great for someone who gets up at four thirty every morning) but also an improved outlook toward life. Your diet truly impacts how you *feel*. Not just how you look.

I know "comfort food" like mac 'n' cheese, biscuits, and fried chicken might make you feel good in the moment, but when they're combined with a body already stressed out from PTSD, it's a deadly combination.

You have to accept that racism impacts your body. A black person in America just can't afford to eat whatever they want, the way white people might. Our bodies are already working against us due to the stress we're pumping into them. We've got to come to terms with that and then embrace a healthier lifestyle.

Another critical element of dealing with PTSD, outside of therapy and diet, is making "quiet time" part of your routine. "One of the most important things you can do when you have PTSD is disconnect from stimulation," states mindbodygreen .com "Make quiet time for yourself a major priority, even if it's just five minutes a day at first."*

Some good ways to disconnect are practices like meditation, yoga, or qigong. Less-structured ways are relaxing activities like gardening, painting, or fishing. Some of those might sound corny or "washed" to you, but you need that calming influence in your life, no matter what your age. A lot of young people

---

*Pam Butler, "These Are the Tools That Helped Me Overcome My PTSD," mindbodygreen, April 1, 2018.

aren't comfortable with silence, but sitting alone to unwind can be incredibly therapeutic. And I don't mean sitting staring at your phone in silence. I mean sitting in silence with your eyes closed so your brain can breathe a bit.

You need a space in your day when you're not staring at a screen and your mind isn't racing. PTSD has your mind stressed, whether you know it or not. You need to do everything within your power to help calm it down.

Blackanoid and PTSD Clinical Correlation by Dr. Ish

From day one until day now there have only ever been two clearly identifiable reasons we as humans do anything. Pleasure and pain: We try to find a way to get away from something painful or to increase the pleasure in our lives. Charlamagne touches on those basic instincts here. Why did we hunt? To avoid being hungry. Why do we seek shelter? To avoid the pain of living in the elements. Why do we marry? It used to be a much more practical matter of avoiding extinction and ensuring the survival of your specific family and ultimately the species. Now it's almost strictly because of a little thing called love; seeking pleasure. All animals' survival instincts are keen, and humans are no different. In fact, humans are hard-wired to give the most pleasurable and the most painful of experiences in our lives the highest priority in our memory banks. And of the two, the painful stimuli are the ones we remember the most vividly because those are the ones that hurt the most and could ultimately threaten the chances of our survival. Our first priority is always to avoid pain.

Appropriately enough, the feeling that we associate the most with any possible painful experience is fear. Lions. Tigers. Bears. Fire. Cold. Water (if you can't swim). Rejection. Disappointment. Being unloved and alone. These are common fears to us all no matter where you come from. As African-Americans we have the dubious distinction of having had the basic list of our primal fears be expanded by our slave experience. Being not enough. Being less than. Being different. Being held back. Being oppressed. Being deprived. Being subjugated. Being unable to control your life in any meaningful way. Being broke. Feeling like no matter what you do, how hard you try, or how fast you run, you'll never be able to run fast enough to outpace the yoke racism places around your neck is a primal fear that was systematically then, and is however overtly or covertly now, instilled in Africans in America, since the day we stepped on the boat. Racism is real, and fear of racism is even more real.

As a psychiatrist who also specializes in children and adolescents, I learned that there are only two fears a child is born with. The fear of falling and the fear of a loud sound. We have to be taught how to be afraid of everything else. Don't touch that stove; it's hot. Don't jump in that water; you might drown. Don't associate with those people over there; they're different . . . and might hurt you. Don't go into that restaurant to eat; there's nobody in there who looks like you. Be afraid. Be safe. Be the same and hope things will change by and by.

A huge take-home lesson from this chapter is Charlamagne's describing our fight-or-flight response. The fight-or-flight or acute-stress response is triggered by just that: a dangerous stressor. It's supposed to turn on and then turn off to serve a protective function to keep you safe. In African-American culture not only has that response been heightened by our traumatic history in this country, but for most of us, it's still in a constant state of hyperarousal because of the ongoing day-to-day stressors we face, real or imagined, for living while being black. Charlamagne touches on the chemistry here, and it is undeniable. Here's how it works. There are two levels of response; one psychological and the other physiological. The body and the mind. The reticular activating system, or RAS for short, is a small network of nerve pathways connecting your spinal cord to your brain, and it is the part of your central nervous system that's responsible for making you aware and alert. It is the gatekeeper that filters all pieces of sensory information from your surroundings and only allows those things that are important to get through to your conscious mind, to make you pay attention, achieve goals, and keep yourself alive. The most painful or pleasurable of things take top priority, like the sound of your name being called, any threat to your safety or the safety of someone you love, and the signs that your partner wants to have sex.*

*"Reticular Activating System: Definition & Function," Study.com, study.com/academy/lesson/reticular-activating-system-definition-function.html.

Top priority. It's biologically wired into our brains. When a threat is perceived, your RAS makes you aware of the danger and that psychological interpretation or fear triggers a physiological reaction. Your adrenal glands, which sit on top of your kidneys, are triggered to release adrenaline. This gets you physically ready to take action. Your heart and breathing rate increase because you're going to need more energy and oxygen. Your pupils dilate so you can become more aware of your immediate surroundings. Blood flow is redirected to your brain, muscles, legs, and arms so you have more power to run or fight. Your skin tenses, and your hairs begin to stand on end. Your blood pressure increases to keep the flow, but your blood itself will now have the ability to clot quicker in case you end up bleeding to help you stay alive. These physiological changes get your body ready to perform under pressure, real or imagined.*

The other stress hormone that's released as a part of this response by your adrenal glands to help you adapt to danger is cortisol. While adrenaline levels will subside naturally over the course of forty minutes, cortisol levels require a release mechanism in order to subside. Get excited and complete a task; cortisol levels subside. Finish the fight—victorious or not; cortisol levels subside. When "the thing" is over, only then will cortisol levels drop. When there's no actual thing to do but a perceived notion there may be, cortisol levels will stay elevated, and that chronic elevation is what causes the damage. Chron-

*Kendra Cherry, "How the Fight or Flight Response Works," *Verywell Mind*, updated June 11, 2018, verywellmind.com/what-is-the-fight-or-flight-response-2795194.

ically elevated cortisol levels cause weight gain, increased blood pressure, increased blood sugar, increased cholesterol, lower immune function, lower levels of learning and memory, and depression. Anything here sound familiar? The very thing that's there to protect you gets stuck in an open cycle or negative-feedback loop and begins to cause you serious long-term harm. Our fear makes us paranoid and, yes, blackanoid of our very own bodies.

Post-traumatic stress disorder is a very common clinical diagnosis in psychiatry and one of the major sources that causes underlying anxiety and panic attacks. PTSD can either be acute due to a recent event or chronic reexperiencing from an event long ago. As a psychiatrist, understanding PTSD helps me understand most of my patients. The *DSM-5* specifically defines PTSD as being "exposed to one or more event(s) that involved death or threatened death, actual or threatened serious injury, or threatened sexual violation."* In addition to the event itself, you have to have experienced it in one or more of the following ways:

- It happened to you.
- You saw it happen to someone else.
- You heard about it happening to a close relative or friend.
- You experienced repeated exposure to distressing details of an event (like a first responder, police officer, medical professional, or rape crisis worker repeatedly seeing or hearing details of a traumatic event).

*Matthew Tull, "DSM-5 PTSD Diagnostic Criteria," *Verywell Mind*, updated June 9, 2018, verywellmind.com/ptsd-in-the-dsm-5-2797324.

That's criterion A. There are also other specific symptoms that need to be experienced across eight different sets of criteria. It sounds complicated but makes sense when you think about the symptoms.

Criterion B says you experience one of the following symptoms associated with the traumatic event: vivid and upsetting memories, nightmares, flashbacks or feeling like you're reliving the actual trauma; triggers that cause you distress (sights, sounds, or smells that remind you of some aspect of the event); or an intense physical reaction when exposed to a reminder of the event, like the fight-or-flight response.

Criterion C describes how we try to avoid any reminders of the event by either avoiding thoughts, feelings, or physical sensations that bring up memories of the trauma or avoiding people, places, conversations, activities, objects, or situations that bring up memories of the trauma—for example, doing everything possible to ensure you don't get pulled over by the police before and while you're driving because the blue lights trigger a panic reaction.

Criterion D in the diagnosis of PTSD has to do with the mood changes that can happen after having at least three of the following symptoms:

- Inability to recall an important aspect of the traumatic event (what soap opera doctors call "amnesia")
- Persistent and heightened negative evaluations about yourself, others, or the world like "People are evil," "I am unlovable," "I'm a bad person," or "The world is not right"
- Heightened sense of guilt, self-blame, or blame of others about the cause or consequences of the event

- Pervasive negative emotional state like shame, anger, or fear
- Anhedonia, or loss of interest in activities that you used to enjoy
- Inability to make personal connections, or feeling detached from others
- Inability to experience positive emotions like love and happiness (what clients often describe as feeling "dead on the inside")

Criterion E has to do with the hypervigilant changes you can experience after an event, including at least three of the following:

- Irritability or aggressive behavior
- Impulsive or self-destructive behavior
- Feeling constantly on edge or on guard or like something bad is about to happen
- Hyper startle response, like loud noises or sudden changes making you jump
- Poor concentration
- Poor sleep

If the aforementioned symptoms last for more than a month, cause you distress, or interfere with your level of functioning at home or work and are not due to a medical condition or substance use, you may have PTSD.

CHAPTER 4

The Fear of Therapy

"We're taught, 'Just go to church and pray about it.
The Lord is going to heal you.' Well, in the meantime,
I believe God-gifted people, physicians, doctors,
therapists—that's your healing. Take advantage of it.
Go see a professional so that they can assess you. It's
okay if you're going through something. Depression
is not okay, but it is okay to go get help."
—Tenitra Michelle Williams

Despite never entering a therapist's office until I was almost
forty, there was a period growing up that I thought I might
actually want to become a shrink.

From early on I've had it in my head that I wanted to help
people with their problems. For some reason folks have always
seemed to come to me with their issues (something that continues to this day). Friends, relatives, classmates, casual acquain-
tances: it seemed like everyone I knew saw me as a good person
to ask for advice and help with what they were going through.

At first I used to think, "How the hell am I supposed to know
how to handle this situation? Why would they bring this to

me?" Over time, however, I realized that they were coming to me because I was a good listener.

That's right, the man who is constantly running his mouth on radio, TV, and podcasts is actually a pretty good listener. In the South, if someone asks you how you're doing, a common reply is, "I'm aright and if I'm not, who is going to listen?" Well, in my circle the answer was "yours truly."

An example of advice that was helpful for more than just the one caller involves a guy I grew up with named Chuck. He was in love with a young lady who he thought had cheated on him. The problem started when DMX and Method Man came to North Charleston for the *Hard Knock Life Tour* in 1999. This was a very big deal for us. So big that I bought a Detroit Tigers starter jacket from Eastbay with the hat to match, blue Enyce jeans, and orange Timberlands just for the show. I thought I was KILLING THEM.

Anyway, we all went to the show together. At some point Chuck got separated from his girl and she ended up backstage with Method Man and DMX. Uh-oh. If you remember the movie *Backstage*, there was a scene with Method Man running through a hotel lobby with a bunch of groupies following him. Well, that was filmed in North Charleston after the show and Chuck's girl was in there somewhere.

According to the rumors that later made their way around town, she ended up smashing DMX after the show. She denied it, but not surprisingly, the rumors drove Chuck crazy. Especially after the movie came out.

Eventually Chuck came to me looking for advice, so I told him you're either going to believe the streets or your girl. If your girl said she didn't sleep with DMX, then you have to believe her. If you choose not to believe her, then you are letting what other people are saying dictate how you feel.

See, the rumor that she slept with DMX came about simply because she told everyone she met him and that he was barking her name. We all just *assumed* X smashed because back then that's what we thought happened when the Dog barked at your girl backstage. But we didn't actually know.

As I told Chuck, not believing her is only going to stress you out, so why choose stress? That's pretty sound advice, right? (The truth is, I don't even know why I chose to tell him that because, in my mind, DMX probably did smash. But we had no proof, so what sense would it make to be upset at someone over a rumor?)

It's a good thing I never pursued being a therapist as I'd probably end up having sex with a lot of my female patients. As someone who in my younger years spent a lot of time giving advice to women, I totally understand how the Dr. Martin Luther King Jr.s and Elijah Muhammads of the world got into so much trouble with the ladies. When a woman is coming to you with her problems and you are genuinely trying to help, there's an inevitable attraction that occurs. It usually starts off mental, then becomes emotional, and sometimes winds up physical. I have no doubt those great leaders were genuinely trying to help, but one thing led to another. At the end of the day I don't care how principled a man you are, you're still a man.

Those concerns aside, I kept on giving so much advice informally that by the time I had a radio show in Columbia, South Carolina, on the Big DM 101.3, I had a segment called "Dr. Charla the Ghetto Psychiatrist." Listeners to my radio show would call in and ask me for help with the normal stuff people would be going through in the hood. One time a guy called and told me that his girlfriend was having an affair with a dog. No, not a man who had a reputation for sleeping around, but having sex with an actual dog. (OK, maybe not so normal.)

I got so used to hearing people's confessions, dreams, fears, and predicaments that after a while I thought, "Man, maybe I'll just open up a psychiatrist office one day." It seemed like a cool job. All I needed was a place with a couch and chair for me to sit in. I was attracted by the idea of getting to run my own business and set my own hours. I figured the pay would be pretty good too.

The problem, besides not being the best student—and being a psychiatrist requires going to medical school—was that I didn't really have any role models to set my sights on. I'm sure there were therapists in Moncks Corner, but I didn't know any, nor did I know anyone who used to go to one. As far as I was concerned the only therapist I knew growing up was the TV character Frasier.

I didn't have any relatable role models in the media either. White America had shows like *Frasier* or *Dr. Phil*. (It felt like every time I turned on *Dr. Phil* there were some white people spilling their guts about something.) But I didn't see any black men out there offering that sort of advice.

Around Moncks Corner, if you did hear the word "therapy," it was probably used in the context of "physical therapy." Hurt your knee playing football? You need physical therapy. Or if someone rear-ended you and you were trying to get a check from their insurance company, then you'd definitely want to go to physical therapy to make sure you had a good case.

You would hear about rehab from time to time. My father

had to go for a stretch, but I never spoke to him about it. We didn't see rehab as a place where people went and worked out their issues. It was more of a punishment imposed by the government that you had to deal with if you wanted to avoid jail.

It's not that we didn't have any exposure to mental health resources. During middle school I was being disruptive, so they put me and a bunch of my friends in a program called SKIP. They would make us sit in a circle and then each one of us would announce why we were there. "Hi, my name is Lenard McKelvey," I would have to say, "and I'm here today because I disrupt class, get into fights, and was caught drinking alcohol at school."

After all the kids had gone around and confessed to whatever ruckus they'd created, a counselor would ask each of us what was behind our behavior. "Do your disruptions stem from a lack of attention at home?" he might ask, or "Do you think about drinking often?"

I had zero interest in taking it seriously. When you're dealing with teenagers, especially boys, you have to talk to them one-on-one if you want to get anywhere. In my experience group therapy is pretty much a waste of time at that age. I can promise you none of us even considered being vulnerable or talking about our problems in front of our peers. Be vulnerable in front of the thirteen-year-old boy you just shared a forty of Olde English with? Unpack your family issues in front of a kid you were going to play basketball with after school? You just knew the jokes were never going to stop flying once you left that classroom. Rather than open up, we all tried to outdo each other in who could take the sessions the *least* seriously.

I grew so out of hand that by the time I got to high school the administration did make me see a counselor one-on-one. It didn't go much better. The guy asked me if I heard voices, and I replied with something to the effect of "Yeah, I hear one asking me stupid questions." The counselor decided there wasn't anything wrong with me other than being a major asshole.

His assessment wasn't wrong, but looking back there's no doubt I could have really benefited from some solid therapy during high school.

Therapy. WTF Is That?

Unlike most of my friends or other members of the community, I didn't hold any bias toward therapy. If anything, I admired the profession. Unfortunately, I wasn't able to make the connection in my mind between what I imagined a therapist to be—someone sitting in a nice chair in an office taking notes while their patient lies in front of them on a couch—with what I had encountered in SKIP, or with that high school counselor. I was also already too invested in being a thug to turn things around at school and put in the time it would have taken.

My positive view on (despite my unengaged relationship with) therapy was a rarity in the African-American community. For most black folks, getting help is a big taboo.

First off, there's always been a lot of suspicion—in some cases even fear—about the practice. Primarily due to the fact that most therapists are white. Not a lot of black folks want to run to a white person with their problems. Especially when the majority of those problems stem from a system organized and run by white people. Seems like a counterintuitive thing to do. You might say, "Stop being so paranoid. Slavery's been over." But you could probably understand why someone Jewish wouldn't want to sit down with a German to discuss the trauma they still feel from the Holocaust. Just as you could understand why an Armenian might not want to see a Turkish therapist, or a Palestinian might not feel comfortable opening up to an Israeli therapist. Well, the same applies to African-Americans and whites.

There is still a basic mistrust of any sort of white-run system that claims it can "help" black people. We still remember the Tuskegee experiment, in which the "doctors" told black share-croppers they were getting free health care, but in reality they were shooting them up with syphilis. Just as black folks saw how housing projects were hyped as a way to provide blacks with cheap, affordable housing but in reality served as a form of government-sponsored segregation. And let's not even get into how the community views police officers whose job it is to "serve and protect" tax-paying African-American citizens. So yeah, we're still a little suspicious.

Because of this mistrust, the way black folks have dealt with their oppression over the years is to handle their business internally. Privately. In the community. Or better yet, in the family. "Don't put your business in the street" is a phrase you hear over and over again. Don't share too much. Don't needlessly expose yourself. Don't give them the rope they can later hang you with. These are attitudes that don't mesh with walking into a stranger's office and baring your deepest emotions.

Outside of suspicion, a lot of folks think therapy just doesn't work. To them, the idea of talking your way through your problems is just more evidence of America becoming too soft. Therapy sounds like something privileged white kids invented just to get out of trouble with their naïve parents. My father was definitely of that mind-set. "That nigga not crazy; he don't need no damn therapist," I once heard him say. "What he need is his ass kicked. That'll get him together." The truth is though that while my father wasn't mentally ill, he probably would have benefited from talking to a licensed professional therapist.

Another factor is that as a society, we can be, well, very black-and-white about things. You're either crazy or sane. Good or evil. Healthy or sick. Right or wrong.

In therapy, things are much more gray. You can be crazy *and* sane, healthy *and* sick, right *and* wrong. You can seem to have your shit together on the outside but still be holding all sort of pain or anxiety on the inside. It's a view of the world that didn't hold much water with a lot of black folks. "That's just the white man poisoning your mind," I could hear someone's auntie say in response to the idea of talking through your problems. "Ain't nothing wrong with you that some prayer can't fix."

Ah, the church. Whenever you're a black person living foul and not moving the way you are supposed to, the community's diagnosis will always be "It's the devil." And their prescription will always be "Get your butt in a church and talk to the Lord."

To good churchgoing people, taking your problems to a therapist, instead of to Jesus, is a sign of a lack of faith. I don't see it that way. I feel like God will position people and events in your life for you for a reason. If you feel compelled to sit down and talk with a therapist, Jesus could very well be guiding your steps. James 2:20 states, "Faith without works is dead," and I think taking your butt to therapy in an attempt to better yourself is an excellent example of the type of work the Bible is talking about. It's work applied to yourself! Spiritual, mental, and emotional maintenance.

• • •

I haven't been a consistent churchgoer myself, but I don't see where there has to be an "either/or" choice between church and therapy. In both settings you're going to hear a positive word. It might be from a pastor in a church, an elder in a kingdom hall, or a minister or imam at the mosque. Or it might be from a therapist sitting in a chair. The basic principle is the same. You talk, and they listen. Then they give you advice based off their experiences. A pastor references scripture the same way a therapist references certain case studies and medical books. The only thing a pastor can't do that a psychiatrist (a therapist who's gone to medical school) can is prescribe medication.

Personally, I've come to look forward to ending the working week by going to therapy every Friday at three. Just as some people enjoy wrapping up their week every Sunday morning in church. I think both rituals are great and full of benefits.

The one thing church has that you can't replicate sitting with a therapist is a sense of community. Praising God is a team sport. Therapy is one-on-one. There's a certain euphoria that comes from feeling the same spirit that everyone else is catching. I guess there might be a degree of that in certain group-counseling situations, but nothing like the spirit you're gonna catch in church.

On the other hand, you won't encounter some of the judgment in therapy you might catch in certain churches. I know Jesus said to love unconditionally, but a lot of Christians seem to have a hard time with that concept. If you have conflicted feelings about your sexuality, or relationships with some of your relatives, or even your view of spirituality, a tight-knit congregation might be a hard place to open up about it.

Don't get me wrong, the church has provided a spiritual foundation for African-Americans for generations. I don't know where many of us would be without it. Institutions that help us get a higher understanding about God are always needed. I just think we also need to add some practices into the mix that help us understand ourselves more.

Drink Away the Pain

Another barrier standing between a lot of African-Americans and therapy is a reliance on self-medication. To be clear, African-Americans aren't the only community that self-medicates. There are people of every race, religion, and creed who turn to alcohol and drugs when they're going through things.

I can only speak for my people though. And black people, we love to get fucked up! Which is crazy because the white man already got us fucked up, but we love getting even more fucked up on top of that. I believe this is due to our collective struggle and trauma over the years. We've needed whatever was available to dull the pain. And as you know, there are a lot more liquor stores in the hood than therapist offices. A LOT.

Growing up, there was never any doubt that people were struggling. It was something that we always understood. We knew our parents were going through it, just as we knew our aunts, uncles, brothers, sisters, neighbors, and classmates were going through it too. We were going through it ourselves. We always understood.

Too many times though, instead of trying to face head-on what was hurting us, our instinct would be to dismiss our pain. "Don't sweat that," someone might say if you mentioned a problem at home. "Just hit this blunt, you'll be straight." If you'd lost someone close to you, a friend might say, "Man, that's rough. Time to crack this bottle of Henny." (I personally prefer Rémy Martin. Hennessy acts like a laxative for me.) Today, it's the reason a lot of these young kids are poppin' Percs. Or sippin' on lean.

In the hood, people rarely address their issues because they stay fucked up all the time. I remember Mobb Deep and Q-Tip had a record called "Drink Away the Pain," which summed up our attitude pretty well: "I think the whole world's going insane / I fill my mind up with liquor, and drink away the pain." Tupac said the same thing in "Lord Knows" when he rapped, "I smoke a blunt to take the pain out." New York to Cali, we all had the same way of "maintaining."

When we were getting fucked up on weed and liquor it was to escape. Same as I'm sure all the fiends who were buying crack from us were looking for an escape too. Or my father sniffing coke for that matter.

We all wanted a brief moment when reality didn't matter. When we could finally forget our messed-up situations for a minute. Usually it was an effective, albeit temporary, way to cope. Except for angry drunks. I really can't stand someone who is mild-mannered most of the time, but put a few Henny and Cokes in them and they start snarling. Like they want to take your head off. Those people are filled with anger they can't control. They don't know the source of it, they just know they are mad and they need to release some of it on the world.

To me, an angry drunk is a person who wants someone to talk to but doesn't know how to ask. They end up in such a rage that they start crying and breaking down and telling their whole life story. That's why therapy is so powerful, because it allows you to get that shit out without the drugs and alcohol and without breaking anything. And if booze is your problem,

Alcoholics Anonymous could be a good form of therapy. It is a group, but it's also free, and I hear there are meetings in just about every town at all times of the day.

Therapy Helps Those Who Help Themselves

It's strange to me that black folks have such a hang-up about asking for assistance when it comes to our emotional issues. In almost every other instance black people have *zero* qualms about asking for help. Black people are usually quick to ask for anything: a job, a date, a ride, five dollars to put toward a bag of weed, you name it. I can't tell you how many brothers come up to me and say, "Yo, Charlamagne, put me on, man!" They're not asking for a specific job or position, they're just asking me to wave a magic wand they seem to think I have and make them famous. No hesitation, no sense of self-consciousness. You need something? Man, you better ask for it! Loudly! With confidence! In the words of Kevin Hart, "Say it with your fucking chest!"

But ask for help when it comes to mental health? Whoa. Slow down. You're tripping.

For too long, emotional help has been the one thing we've been uptight asking for. Even though we know—to a person—that the pain is there. I doubt there's an African-American reading this book who isn't somehow connected to that pain. Even if their own life is on track, there's someone in their world—a parent, a sibling, a close friend—who is struggling emotionally. Who is silently suffering as a black person in America. Yet still isn't asking for help. But it's like Zora Neale Hurston said almost a hundred years ago: "If you are silent about your pain, they'll kill you and say you enjoyed it."

We can't be silent any longer. Especially when a lot of that pain is being inflicted on us by others. Thankfully, I'm beginning to sense a change. I hear people talking about therapy. Openly. Without embarrassment. Offhandedly, even. Maybe it's because now that I'm in sessions myself people are sharing with me. Telling me that they are currently going, or they want to in the future. The same way someone might say, "Yeah, man, I need to get back in the gym," now they'll say, "Yeah, I need to link up with a therapist." Really, there's not much difference. The gym helps you get your body right. The therapist helps you get your mind right. It doesn't even make sense that you would celebrate one and shy away from the other. They're both great ideas.

We all share so many of the same fears and insecurities. I have friends who might have grown up in the Bronx, or Detroit, or LA, maybe even during different eras, but when we talk about it, we see that we often share the exact same pain and the exact same trauma. And once we can admit that, the pain that used to feel so heavy suddenly begins to lift. We are actually able to laugh about a lot of this because we've all been through it. We realize it's not just us alone on an island.

And if you're still hearing that old refrain "Don't put your business in the streets" ringing in your head, remember confidentiality is one of the cornerstones of therapy. Knowing that you can say anything to your therapist and it will stay in the room helps you to build trust to open up. All therapists are legally and ethically bound to keep their sessions confidential and not discuss them with anyone else. Basically, they have a no-snitching policy!

You Don't Choose a Therapist;
a Therapist Chooses You

The first thing a lot of people ask me is, "when is the right time to go?" I don't know if there's a one-size-fits-all answer, since so much depends on your personal situation.

I can say this: for me, approaching forty felt like the perfect time to start unpacking my life. I've always been someone who trusts my instincts, and a couple of years ago my instincts told me, "Time to let go of some of this baggage you've been carrying around." Time to let go of a lot of attachments and fears that I've been needlessly letting weigh me down.

In the past, whenever I felt unsure of myself, I trusted that I had mentors to lean on. Two very impactful ones were Dr. Robert Evans and the Honorable Minister Louis Farrakhan. People I could go to for guidance and wisdom. But as I began to become more and more successful, I noticed a shift in my relationships. Instead of finding mentors, I was becoming the mentor to a younger generation. People wanted to ask me for advice. I was becoming a go-to guy for a lot of people. And I loved helping them. But as I always say, "Who does the go-to guy go to?" For me, the answer was a therapist.

That was my path. But by no means do I think you need to wait until you're approaching middle age to talk to a therapist. High school kids need someone to talk to. College kids definitely need someone to talk to, especially if you're going to a school that's taking you outside of your comfort zone and exposing you to different people and ways of life. I've never been to college, but I have to assume that it can create a lot of anxiety and insecurity. Most colleges provide mental health counseling. If you feel like you need it, take advantage of it.

It's no different if you're just starting out in your career. You should still definitely try to find mentors and OGs in your profession who can guide you and help you avoid pitfalls. But that might not be enough. Your OG can show you every shortcut and help you make the right connections, but if you're weighed down by a lot of unnecessary emotional baggage, you're still going to struggle to get there. Maybe even waste valuable years running in place instead of getting where you're trying to go.

Be honest with yourself. If you're young and ambitious but struggling with anxiety, make therapy a priority. I know, when you're just starting out, funds are tight. Therapy might not seem like a necessary expenditure. But if you need it, it damn sure is. Probably the very best way you could spend the money.

In fact, let's talk about how much therapy costs, since it's an issue that stops a lot of folks before they ever get started. I won't lie, on the surface therapy seems expensive. Personally, I pay $150 for an hour-long session. I do it out near my house in New Jersey, but if I was doing it in Manhattan it might crack $300.

Nationally prices tend to range between $75–$100 per session. I know if you're on a budget, that might seem like an astronomical price. "Four hundred dollars a month?" you might be screaming. "That's more than my car note!" I get it. It's a lot of money.

But I also promise you it's a fantastic investment. Because you're investing in *yourself*. Getting your mind right is going to get you a lot further, and make you a lot more attractive, than a new pair of Yeezys. Or having an updated iPhone. Or buying a new pair of distressed jeans. (By the way what's up with buying brand-new jeans that look raggy? Why do your jeans look like your emotional state, all worn and tired? Your jeans look like they need some form of therapy.)

If you have insurance, call up your provider and see what sort of therapy they cover. Most insurance companies provide at least some level of coverage, though a lot of them set a limit on how many sessions they'll pay for over the course of the year. Take advantage of that coverage if you have it. Even if your insurance won't pay for all your sessions, they can at least put a big dent in your overall bill.

If doing therapy weekly is simply out of the question financially, then start only going once a month. If you start seeing the results, and I expect you will, it will become easier for you to prioritize weekly sessions in your budget. You'll start to see why it is actually more beneficial than new shoes, or going out to eat all the time.

If you don't have health insurance many therapists also work on what's known as a sliding-scale model. That means they take your yearly income into account and charge you according to what they think you can afford. So while I might have to pay a therapist $150, someone else might be able to get sessions with the same person for $75, or even $50. A lot of shrinks don't advertise that they'll use a sliding scale, so it might be on you to speak up and ask if it's a possibility. Don't be shy about it—it's very standard in the industry, and even if it turns out not to be an option, you're not playing yourself by asking.

There are even some therapists who are willing to work pro bono, which basically means for free. Again, they're not going to advertise that, but if you have a compelling case on why you need therapy but can't afford it, don't be afraid to ask. Most are empathetic people by nature, so chances are they'll at least listen to you. If they don't work pro bono, maybe they'll recommend a colleague who does. If having an African-American therapist is important to you and you don't know where to start, you can check out africanamericantherapists.com, which is a national list of black therapists, counselors, and psychologists. You can also check out psychologytoday.com, which keeps a searchable database of African-American therapists. Therapyforblackgirls.com also has a really helpful listing of African-American therapists by state, as well as a cool podcast about the experience of getting therapy.

You might also check out online therapy sites like Talkspace that allow you to talk with a shrink at cheaper prices than you would for an office visit. I personally like sitting down face-to-face with someone, but online therapy might be a way for you to at least get your foot in the door and start experiencing the benefits.

Another option is group therapy. In addition to Alcoholics Anonymous or Narcotics Anonymous, there is the group Beyond Addiction. There are plenty of group therapies designed to offer more general counseling and support. And they usually cost about a quarter of what individual sessions run. If you think you'd be uncomfortable talking about your issues in front of other people, try out a session and see how it goes. You don't have to say anything if you're not feeling it. At worst, you've sat there for an hour and listened to other people talk. You've wasted plenty of other hours in your life. Giving this a shot won't kill you. But if you do happen to like the setup, it could be a very cost-effective way for you to get the support you need.

Also, if you're worried about money, be sure to contact local hospitals and community agencies. Many of them offer low-cost—or free—therapy with graduate students who are working toward getting their therapist license. Yes, you might get someone whose still figuring out their approach and style, but there's really no downside to it. At the very least you're getting someone to talk to and work things out with. And often the students are supervised by a licensed therapist, so you might actually end up getting two smart people helping you for the price of one!

How to Choose a Therapist by Dr. Ish

The road to living your best emotional life is full of challenges, and it takes real courage to decide you need to find a professional to help with this. Unfortunately it can feel intimidating to choose from all the different types of therapists. Hopefully this section will ease some of the anxiety. There are three main categories here to consider: psychiatrist, psychologist, and counselor. Big differences between the three. First, understand that all three can be highly trained therapists. Now, let's take a closer look at what each actually does.

A psychiatrist is a medical doctor, or MD, who went to college, then medical school, then residency, and is trained as a general practitioner but specializes in psychiatry or mental health. Their primary function is to restore brain balance in terms of neurotransmitters and chemicals and as such are qualified across the board to write you a prescription in the efforts to help you do so. Depression, anxiety, post-traumatic stress disorder, bipolar dis-order, schizophrenia, and ADHD are some of the main diagnoses they treat. In addition to prescribing medications, some psychiatrists are uniquely trained to do therapy as well. A psychiatrist's knowledge is broad in terms of being able to pull from the nearly three hundred diagnoses in the mental health diagnostic manual or *DSM-5* and identify exactly what diagnosis pertains to you.

A psychologist, by contrast, is not a medical doctor but he or she went to college, then graduate school, and has a doctoral degree and is just as highly trained in mental health and oftentimes is a damn sight better at therapy. They are masters at behavior modification and are uniquely qualified to help you break pathological patterns, change old dysfunctional behaviors, and shape new productive behavior. Typically a psychologist will only do therapy, but in certain states some are qualified to write prescriptions as well. If a psychiatrist's knowledge base is broad, a psychologist's is deep and highly specialized.

A counselor is exactly that, your wise counsel. They went to college and likely majored in psychology or social work and obtained a master's degree or became licensed to perform therapy. So they're not as specialized as the other two but are much more readily available and accessible in terms of providing you care. Your counselor's primary function is providing you support and guidance while teaching you specific life-building skills along the way in all areas of mental health. Counselors only perform therapy. Counselors *do not* write prescriptions, and if any of them ever offer you one: run! A counselor generally uses more basic therapeutic techniques to help you with a wide range of life issues. When you hear someone say, "I have my therapist on speed dial," they're usually referring to a counselor.

A common misperception and big point to understand is that among the three, they all can be considered your therapist as they all can be trained in specific therapeutic techniques. It's rare to find a psychiatrist who's equally as well trained in therapy, but in the event you do: keep them!

Often people will start with a counselor and if there's no improvement they'll go to a psychologist. If your psychologist determines there may be an underlying chemical imbalance, they'll often refer you to a psychiatrist. But the reverse also happens where people's primary care doctor will refer them directly to a psychiatrist for treatment, then the psychiatrist will uncover pathological patterns or major life issues that will require more in-depth therapy to resolve. You can get better with either medications or therapy, but the secret sauce to your cure lies in doing a bit of both. Depending on what issue you're working through, medications can help you from hitting rock bottom while you get to work on processing your underlying emotions and learning new life skills.

Goodness of Fit

Once you figure out the specific type of professional, the next thing to consider is goodness of fit, which is equally important. It's best to get a recommendation for a couple of reasons: One, it's a small community, and within that community of professionals we know who's good and who's not. And two, depending on who's referring you to whom, they'll have a feel for what you specifically need in terms of therapy or meds or both and get you to the right person. All mental health professionals have specific areas of focus or areas they're much better at than most, and that reputation is known in the community as well, so take advantage of that. It's best to see at least two or three before you settle on one. If I may use a relationship analogy, you want to consider this your "I'm dating people but no one exclusively just yet" phase. Date around; you'll know the right fit when you meet them because you'll feel connected, you'll feel like they listen to you, and you'll feel like they genuinely care about helping you with your problem. If you don't feel those things when you're in their office, you're in the wrong office.

There are some key areas you want to take into account before deciding on who's going to be your provider or providers (because people often have both a psychiatrist and a therapist or counselor) that you wouldn't think make a difference but in actuality can be huge. Gender. Depending on what you've been through, particularly if it's a sexual trauma, you may be naturally more comfortable with a male or female. Sometimes your referral will be made based on that or based on whom you *need* to become more comfortable with to move forward in life. Also, their age is a huge factor. Again, in certain cases it may be best to pick someone older than you, particularly if there may be some old unresolved mommy or daddy issues. Even though it shouldn't be, obviously ethnicity can play a factor. It helps if you both speak the same language and get some of the same cultural cues. Some people are just more comfortable opening up to someone who looks like them. They tend to feel that person "gets them" even though the opposite may be true. This is a particular problem in the African-American community because, as a whole, we don't seek mental health treatment nearly as much as other ethnicities, and when we do the chances of us finding somebody in the chair who actually looks like us are slim . . . especially an African-American male. So if that's what you're looking for and you hit the lottery and find one who's good, stay right there; you're home.

Outside of those genetic match factors there are other things you want to know. For certain you want to know their area of specialty in terms of what they treat and what techniques they use. Every mental health professional can treat you for most issues but will customarily have a specific area of focus where they're proficient. Trauma? Depression? Panic attacks? Mood swings? Personality issues? They usually specify on their website and use that area of specialty as their calling card. Also you want to be aware of the different therapeutic techniques or psychotherapy your provider has at their disposal. The most common type of therapy is supportive therapy because when we're not feeling our best that's the most common thing we need: support. Supportive therapy consists primarily of active listening and of varying degrees of comforting, encouraging, reassuring, and advising. Just knowing someone is there and is giving you their undivided attention relays a sense of significance, and that goes a long way.

Cognitive behavioral therapy, or CBT, is the next most common type of therapy and consists primarily of your therapist challenging your automatic, and often wrong, assumptions about yourself and how the world in which you live works. The goal is to break your dysfunctional patterns by helping you consciously decide what you want to think, feel, and do in any given situation. Thoughts control your emotions. Your emotions control your behavior. Behaviors control your actions. You actions shape your life. Important stuff, so don't leave it to chance.

Then there's the classic free-association-type therapy or Freudian psychoanalysis that we've all seen on TV. You come into the office, sit or sometimes lie back on their couch, they say, "So, tell me about your mother," and off you go freely associating while they're connecting the dots. The main thrust here is to uncover the root causes of your emotional conflict and identify exactly why you think the things you think and do the things you do, with the ultimate goal of giving you control to direct those things once you're made aware.

Outside of those factors there are definitely more practical things to think about. Access. Does my insurance cover these visits? A quick call to your carrier can clear that up. Also, what are the professional's specific practice rules of engagement? How and how often can you contact them? Visits per month? Calls per week? Texts per day? Email whenever? Their office staff can inform you of that when you call for an appointment. Be honest with yourself, and if their program doesn't sound like it fits your needs, call someone else.

Last, you want to consider length of treatment. Traditional psychoanalysis can last for years, but in this day and age, to quote Sweet Brown, "Ain't nobody got time for that!" and quite honestly, it's very likely not necessary. Consider brief psychotherapy, when there's one specific issue you need to move past and that can last anywhere from one to three months. Problem-focused or behavioral modification therapy is best for a cluster of symptoms and can last up to a year. Supportive therapy is just that, surrogate support, and can last indefinitely, until you feel like you're ready to walk it like you talk it.

I think the most crucial thing to consider when trying to find a good therapeutic fit is to find someone who you feel listens to you and genuinely cares about you doing better. They're there to lend your ego strength and believe in you until you're ready to start believing in yourself. Just like there's the perfect person out there for you to love, there's also a perfect mental health professional out there waiting to help you heal.

My Therapist Is a White Woman

No disrespect to Dr. Ish, but when I decided to see a therapist I wasn't as concerned by whether they were a psychologist or a psychiatrist, I just knew I didn't want a black therapist. No, not because I hate myself and want to bleach my skin white. I just wanted to sit down with someone who felt like my opposite.

My reasoning was that I wanted someone who didn't have the same experience as me. I didn't want them to have the same biases and preconceived notions that I do about situations.

That might sound like it runs counter to everything I've been saying so far, but I wanted my sessions to be unique. I wanted them to be about me. I wanted someone who was going to be listening to me in a vacuum, instead of associating me with their own experiences.

I didn't want someone black, and I didn't want a man, but I also didn't want a white woman. So I initially set my sights on an Asian therapist. I booked an appointment with an Asian woman in New Jersey, but while I was waiting for that session, my assistant told me she went online and found a highly reviewed psychologist just fifteen minutes from my house with an immediate opening. Only issue was that she was a white woman.

I can't lie, since my schedule is so hectic, being that close to my house was a big attraction. It's not that different from picking out a gym. It's helpful if it's close to your home or work. I decided to give her a shot. I wasn't expecting much, but lo and behold, I liked this woman's energy. I value energy above everything else, so that was huge for me. But what really sold me on her was that she keeps a big bowl of Werther's Original caramel candies in her office. I've always loved Werther's Originals because they remind me of my grandmother. She would have those at the house when I was a kid, so just the sight of them brought me immediate comfort and helped me feel relaxed.

Despite my preconceived notions, I decided to stick with the good energy and classic candies. It just felt right to me. And now, every Friday I look forward to sitting down with my white therapist and unpacking my life. I've found the best thing about talking to a white therapist is that it's one of the few times a white person is actually shutting the fuck up and *listening* to the issues that we face as black Americans.

The way I see it, not only am I benefiting from the sessions, but maybe, just maybe, these interactions will change how my therapist sees things. In turn, she'll talk to other white people, and in time it could lead to more white people using their privilege to combat prejudice. To truly attempt to be a part of the solution to the problem white people's ancestors created and benefit from today. In the words of the great urban philosopher Doughboy from *Boyz n the Hood*, "Either they don't know, don't show, or don't care about what's going on in the hood," so those one-on-one interactions between black people and white people at the therapist's office do just as much for them as they do for us.

Now maybe you're a little bit blacker than me and a bowl of candies isn't enough to make you feel comfortable spilling your guts to a white person. I respect that. If that's the case, then you should look into finding a therapist who looks like you and might have a little bit more insight into your experience. Plus, it's great to support a black business, especially a small one.

Be warned though, there aren't nearly as many black therapists out there. According to the American Psychological Association, just 2 percent of its members are African-American.

But you can still find them. *Psychology Today* has a national listing of African-American therapists on its website. The Association of Black Psychologists has a listing of members on its website as well. And online therapy options like Talkspace allow you to request therapists by race and gender.

If for some reason you aren't able to find a black therapist, or one you vibe with, please don't let that be the obstacle that stops you from getting help. You might have to go out of your comfort zone both emotionally and physically. If circumstances dictate it, you might have to drive to the white folks' neighborhood to meet your therapist. If that's that case, don't feel uncomfortable. Don't feel like you're somewhere you're not supposed to be. Getting help is your right. If it helps, remember that one of the reasons the neighborhood is so nice in the first place is because a lot of the people there have access to therapy. They collectively have their shit together. So instead of being intimidated, grab a little bit of that community's energy and take it back to the hood with you.

Do You Know What Therapy Looks Like?

I've been talking a lot about why you should try therapy, but I want to highlight what an actual session is like. Because therapy is such a private moment, you don't ever hear too much about how those sixty minutes play out. We've seen little glimpses of sessions on shows like *The Sopranos*, or in movies like *Antwone Fisher* and *Good Will Hunting*. But very few people have a real sense of what happens, for the most part because most folks aren't going to go into much detail about their session. Luckily, I'm not most folks, and I'm pretty comfortable sharing personal things. So this is how it goes for me:

My therapist's office is in a space she shares with other therapists. There's a little waiting room I sit in from when I arrive until she comes out to greet me. (Pro tip: You want to arrive for your appointment on time. Therapists rarely let a session go over, so they usually run on schedule. If you show up for an appointment from 3:00–3:45 at 3:15, you're probably only getting a half hour but will still have to pay for the whole thing.)

Once I get into her room, the setup is warm. That's the best way to describe it. It's always dimly lit in a comfortable way. I remove my coat if I have one and sit on her couch to talk. She sits in a recliner about five feet away, facing me. There's a little glass table with the candies between us. I know there's the classic image of lying down on your therapist's couch, but I don't like talking to people while I'm lying down unless I'm in bed with my wife. Or maybe on a beach chair. Overall, I don't feel really engaged when I'm lying down. I prefer to look straight at someone and have the conversation face-to-face.

Then we start talking.

She'll usually start the conversation by asking me how my week was, but generally she doesn't lead me too much. If I ask her a question she'll respond, but there are plenty of times I'll say something and she'll let my words hang there, without a response. She's never explained why, but I've noticed that when she does that, it forces me to go deeper into whatever subject I'm talking about.

I've become comfortable driving the conversation, but if you're black, it might take some getting used to. Black folks are used to getting a lot of affirmations during their monologues. If you're black and tell someone, "And then I told him I wasn't trying to hear that," the person I'm talking to might say, "Damn straight," or "I know that's right . . ." If the person you're talking to doesn't say anything, it might actually throw you off. You might think, "Is this person even listening to me?"

In therapy they're definitely listening, but don't expect much in the way of feedback or encouragement. Chances are your therapist isn't going to say, "That's right," or "Word," every time you tell them something. You're going to put stuff out there, and they might not say anything back in return. They'll just wait for you to keep going. Don't get thrown off by that. Embrace the silence and keep digging deeper. Like the Philadelphia 76ers star Joel Embiid says, "Trust the process."

If you feel like your therapist is either talking too much or not enough, then discuss it with them. It's a perfectly legitimate thing to bring up. If you don't like the way a trainer is working you out, you would say something. Or you would tell a massage therapist to either go softer or harder. It's not different with a therapist. The session is about you, and in all likelihood you're paying a pretty penny for it. If you want the style of the session adjusted, you can say so. If you do and you feel like your therapist was offended, then they're probably not the right person to be your therapist. But please, don't quit on the process. Accept this wasn't a good fit, and then start looking for someone else. A friend recently told me she met with four different therapists before she found the right fit. Now she goes every week and considers therapy, along with losing forty pounds, the most impactful thing she's done for her overall heath and wellness.

I think it's also important to remember that you're not trying to be friends with your therapist. Your mission isn't to impress them, or paint the best picture of yourself. Don't censor yourself because you worried about what your therapist might "think of you."

I still struggle with that from time to time. I'll catch myself getting in my head and worrying, "Man, what is this woman thinking about me?" She's an older white woman, and I wonder if I'm scaring her with my tales from the hood. In the end, I trust that she's professional and she's just there to help.

Those little worries aside, I really look forward to my session each Friday afternoon. To be prepared, I keep notes of things that bother me during the week so we'll have relevant things to discuss. (This is a practice I believe will make your sessions much more effective. Everyone has things that bother them each week. Keep a little notebook by your bed and write them down before you go to sleep. When you review them at your session, you might see there are patterns to what's bothering you.)

I'll also jot down unresolved issues from my past that I feel are still weighing on me.

Currently, one of the things I'm discussing with her is my father leaving my mother for another woman. Some others are my inability to confront death. Getting molested as a child. Regret over the crimes I committed. I'm going to talk about many of these issues in greater detail in subsequent chapters, but for now suffice it to say that they are far from unique. I know a lot of folks with almost the exact same issues.

The problem is that as a community, we aren't dealing with them. We are just taught that it's normal and we've got to learn to "live with it." But why would you want to live with something that is literally killing you? Holding on to all that trauma of the past is killing us slowly, eating away at our spirits, and poisoning our bodies. It's also hard on our relationships and our kids. We end up taking shit out on people we are close to because we don't have a good way to unpack these things. That's why I love venting to my therapist, dumping all this old stuff on her that I should have gotten out years ago. This is yet another reason why a therapist is great, because who else can you get to help you unpack all the old baggage you're still carrying around with you? It's very important that you have that person in your life. Like Erykah Badu said in "Bag Lady": *Bag lady, you gone hurt your back/Dragging all them bags like that/I guess nobody ever told you/All you must hold on to, is you.*

I know therapy is working because when I don't go people around me can always tell. Recently I was out of town and missed two straight sessions. Man, I was so stressed. Everything that was happening in my professional life had me completely riled up. I was on the phone with Angela Rye running my mouth about everything that was going on when suddenly she cut me off.

"You haven't been to therapy, have you?" she asked.

"Nope," I replied, and then it hit me how stressed I really was. I wasn't even conscious of it, but I had been feeling so much anxiety. And that was after missing only two sessions! It pains me to even think about how much stress I had been carrying around all those years I wasn't going to therapy at all!

The Fear of Therapy
Clinical Correlation
by Dr. Ish

This chapter offers a much-needed fresh take on an age-old problem. Black people don't go to therapy. African-American women maybe and much more likely these days, but African-American men, forget about it. Out of the 350 private clients I'm currently seeing, three of them are African-American males. It just doesn't happen, and there are a lot of reasons why that is that need to be examined.

The first of which is that as hard as it is to believe, therapy is still a big taboo in the black community for many reasons. There's an inherent distrust of the process and an irrational fear of what negative consequences could arise as a result of sharing "too much" of your world with a stranger in a perceived authority position. Is it possible you could let something slip in therapy and they, in turn, have to alert "the authorities" like the Department of Social Services, APS, local police, or otherwise to your activities? Extremely rare. The goal is to help you correct those maladaptive patterns of behavior before any of those agencies ever have to become a part of your life. There's also this deep-seated notion in our community that admitting to having any emotional issues, to each other or to ourselves, is a sign of weakness or "being soft." As black men and women we want to see and desperately need to believe that we in fact are strong because our strength can, in turn, help us get through our tough days. It actually doesn't. It just delays the process of us truly healing and moving forward. You can't heal what you're scared to reveal, and in being fearful of being transparent we miss the tremendous opportunity for personal growth. A common therapeutic practice is to break you down before building you back up. As African-Americans, some of us already feel so beaten down we just want to avoid feeling any worse. But in avoiding our issues we miss the healing, growth, and empowerment that come on the other side of a breakthrough. The other bit of pushback that I see from people who have tried and failed to find a connection with a good therapist is that they say, "They just didn't understand me," or "They didn't seem to really care." Fair criticism and one that as a professional working on the inside I get just as frustrated with. To my horror I've found over the years that there is an all too frequent basic lack of cultural competency when it comes to white therapists helping African-American clients, especially young black men. We are consistently misdiagnosed with labels like "conduct disorder," "oppositional defiant disorder," and "schizophrenia." Either we're a behavioral problem or psychotic, which is nonsense. I've also seen there is a general lack of understanding of our cultural cues and mannerisms, how we connect interpersonally and what we actually respond to in terms of feedback. From the first day of my psychiatry residency to the last I was lucky enough to have as my mentor the first African-American psychologist in South Carolina, Dr. Jerome Hanley. He was brilliant, compassionate, and ever vigilant about making sure every mental health professional understood who we were as a people and why. I still smile remembering the night he brought actual slave chains to a doctors' dinner meeting and dropped them on the table. Everybody was shook. He believed it was our duty as African-American mental health professionals to help ensure that the very real social constructs of economics, politics, and race didn't continue to shackle or limit the lives of the people we are here to care for.

While our technology does have the tendency to loosen our actual connections to each other, there are some very cool therapy apps that are helping to bridge the gap. The Talkspace app in particular can be as anonymous or personal as you're comfortable with, and if you're just starting to be exposed to therapy this may be an excellent entry point to getting the help you need.

The other thing we fail to take into account when considering why we've traditionally been so averse to therapy is the conditioning we've received. Africans in America were forced to grow accustomed to a very different type of "therapy" since we've been here. The lash-and-the-whip therapy. Again, we live what we learn. If that's what's done to us, nine times out of ten that's what we're going to do to others. Not because we don't know it's not right, but because it's just the only thing we know. Our foreparents learned to handle us, their children, with the same coarseness with which they themselves were handled. No talking. Just whipping. Just like every family needs a hero, so does every culture. Charlamagne is giving a much-needed voice in helping us find the courage to help ourselves.

Another takeaway from this chapter in terms of our barriers to treatment is the way we judge each other. As African-Americans culturally we've been taught to notice and exaggerate the small differences in each other rather than embrace what's the same. Old versus young. Light-skinned versus dark-skinned. Muscular versus skinny. Smart versus not so smart. Clean-cut versus thug. Weak versus strong. It leads to a very deliberate black-and-white way of relating to each other and doesn't allow room for a lot of acceptance or emotional currency. One of my favorite tenets of psychiatry is that "two things can be true." Charlamagne drives this point home. You can be right and wrong. You can have both positive and negative qualities. You can be both loving and callous. You can be a good man and still cheat. One thing doesn't necessarily cancel out the other. In our community we're quick to pass judgment on and write each other off rather than take the time to sit and be still with the deeper issues because they make us uncomfortable. Once someone in the community suspects you or a family member may be in therapy there's a whole laundry list of negative judgments they may attribute to you. The saddest part about that is that oftentimes, they have or someone close to them has been struggling with the exact same challenge but afraid to face it. So instead of standing out and doing the thing that takes courage, the natural psychological inclination is to desperately try to fit back in and do what everybody else does. We self-medicate with alcohol, marijuana, or pills. We manufacture other behavioral distractions or focus on other people's problems just so we don't have to deal with the problems of the person looking back at us in the mirror. Short-term fixes for long-term problems only lead to more long-term problems. We have to find a way to let each other know that it's OK to have issues and look to someone outside the community for help. One of the first things I tell every new client who's reluctant about therapy is this: "If the people you know and the things you've been doing to fix this problem were working, you wouldn't be here. It's time to try a new way."

CHAPTER 5

Losing My Roots

"I think everyone should do therapy regardless of what you do. . . . Hip-hop was built on telling the truth and being honest with yourself. It was meant to be therapeutic."

—Logic

I've spent the last twenty-some years working like hell to overcome my humble beginnings. I grew up in a single-wide trailer on a dirt road in a small town where the most exciting thing to do on a Saturday night was get fucked up and walk around the local Walmart. I was a young black male in a southern state where the Confederate flag still flew over the state house and being black could get you killed if you weren't careful. I got kicked out of two high schools and never went to college. I was fired from four radio jobs before I finally landed at *The Breakfast Club*.

Those are hurdles that would have knocked a lot of people down. I managed to rise above them. Today I can say I'm one of the most successful radio hosts in the country. All praises due to God. Plus I'm building a media empire that one day I hope will rival those of my media idols like Steve Harvey and Ryan Seacrest.

I'm in a fantastic spot in life.

And for some reason that scares the shit out of me.

I'm not frightened by the temptation of drugs or alcohol. I'm not worried about my access to available women (OK, not anymore since I am a member of the faithful Black Male Association). I'm not even that concerned about making more money—my bank account already has way more zeroes than I ever imagined it would.

No, one of the aspects of fame that's proving the most difficult to navigate is wanting to stay connected to my roots. Will losing my link to home also lead me to lose my sense of self? It's a difficult question, because I'm not 100 percent sure exactly who I am in the first place.

I believe a lot of African-Americans feel a similar anxiety. Either consciously or subconsciously. As a people, we talk a lot about "black culture." But I'm not sure any of us really know what that is. It sure isn't Black Twitter. Culture, by definition, represents "manifestations of human intellectual achievement." While I concede that Black Twitter has produced some fire GIFs and memes, and has also brought awareness to the injustices that black and brown people face at the hands of the police, overall I don't think social media represents our intellectual achievement. If anything, it's collectively making us dumber.

Don't get me wrong, over the centuries African-Americans have done an amazing job of creating cultural content in America. From jazz to blues to hip-hop, we've created something beautiful out of our collective pain, emotions that have resonated throughout the world. America made us start at the bottom of the ladder and then put a foot on our head whenever we tried to climb up a rung. We managed to succeed largely off the strength of our content. To quote our biracial brother from *The 6*, "We started from the bottom now we here!"

Let's take the current state of rap. The white man couldn't stop hip-hop if he tried. He did, however, manage to pacify it. When rap started out, you had young brothers and sisters from the street getting paid by talking about subjects that were conscious and had socially redeeming value. They were creating songs that planted positive seeds in young people's minds. I know because I was one of those young people. Artists like Rakim, Public Enemy, Wu-Tang Clan, Boogie Down Productions, Outkast, and Goodie Mob did so much to expand my intelligence and consciousness.

Then in the 1990s and 2000s the landscape changed. I've worked in radio awhile now and I've come to believe that there are forces that encourage rappers toward lyrics about violence, drugs, guns, money, and degrading women instead of the knowledge the old-school MCs were dropping. Negative energy, which is destroying our communities. It's troubling because I believe if rappers today thought they could get paid from being positive, they would.

They don't believe that though. They can sense that there are forces out there that would prefer they stay negative. Those forces are much more comfortable with rappers talking about how many Lambos are in their driveways or Guccis in their closets, instead of talking about revolutionary figures like Marcus Garvey and Malcolm X. The kind of names I was used to hearing in songs. All that respect for history and philosophy has disappeared. Which is a damn shame, because hip-hop brings people together like weed and alcohol. Imagine if all those young people, having been brought together, were encouraged to study real history and asked tough questions about what our government has done to people. What would happen then? A lot of people currently in power would find themselves out on their asses.

Ultimately, as impactful as jazz, the blues, rock 'n' roll (of course we invented that too), and hip-hop have all been, they have always been viewed through the prism of white America. We danced jigs because the slave masters wouldn't let us cross our feet. We sang the blues because life as a sharecropper was so tough. We created jazz because we were shut out of the classical-music conservatories. We created hip-hop because no one would listen when we tried to tell them just how bad things were in the hood.

Today we're starving for a purer form of culture. A culture that isn't a reaction to how white people have treated us. That's why we gravitated so strongly to *Black Panther*. As soon as that movie came out you saw black folks all around the country doing the "Wakanda Forever" handshakes and calling white folks "colonizers." We want to touch our African roots so bad that even a fictitious homeland feels more real to us than what we have here.

When I heard stories about Africa growing up, they made sense to me. When I read the Grimms' fairy tales I understood them, but I couldn't *feel* them. When I heard African fairy tales like "The Tortoise and the Hare," or "The Monkey and the Shark," man, I felt those stories all the way to my soul. Those stories let me know that no matter what our conditions were here in America, we were descended from something greater. That we were capable of telling our own history and sharing our own wisdom.

I probably felt that connection strongly because I grew up in the Low Country. That's an area spanning the Carolinas where the African culture brought there by slaves hasn't been diluted nearly as much as it has in the rest of the country. A lot of folks in South Carolina are Geechee, which, if you don't already know, refers to descendants of slaves who lived along the Low Country and still speak a dialect that's closer to some African languages than English.

Recently I visited Charleston's future site of the International African American Museum, which will honor the victims of the Middle Passage. It's going to be built on what was once Gadsden's Wharf, which is where almost 50 percent of African slaves entered this country. If you look at a map, you can see why the port had so much traffic. It's pretty much a straight shot from Charleston to West Africa.

The museum is set to open in 2020 and my hope is that one day it will be as popular as Ellis Island. It sure as hell deserves to be. The hundreds of thousands of Africans who were brought to Charleston literally lost everything—their freedom, their families, their homes, their cultures, their languages, and, in many cases, their lives. Yet out of all that misery and loss, their descendants have been able to build new legacies.

Standing by the water and feeling the presence of my ancestors in the air helped me remember one thing: we might have been brought here as slaves, but we didn't start off in this world that way. That's a seemingly obvious point, but it's also one that can get lost in the white man's version of *his*tory. The history books start with us in bondage. They don't teach us about the thousands of years before that. The years during which we were kings and queens and built empires. In which we traded with nations all over the world and created libraries and universities. It's almost as if the story we've been told starts in the fifth or sixth chapter of a book. I want us to be able to go back and read the foreword, the introduction, and all the opening chapters so we can put our experience in context. Our story didn't start with being kidnapped and sold. And it's not going to end with us being second-class citizens either.

Where I'm From

Learning the truth about my roots is becoming a passion as I grow older. I refuse to only think of myself within the context of "black," "Southern," or "American." It's too limiting.

Imagine an Irish-American guy from Michigan only being able to frame himself within the context of "white," or "the Midwest." That would make him feel like something was missing in his story. He probably thrives off being aware of his Irish heritage, even if he only celebrates it on Saint Patrick's Day. Just knowing it's there gives him a sense of identity. A sense of self that's deeper than America.

I want the same thing for myself and my family. That's why I'm so excited to learn what the white man has tried to conceal from me all these years. I'm not just "black," but I've learned I'm Balanta, Mandinka, and Mende. Real peoples with real cultures.

I want to visit the areas those tribes come from. I want to experience those cultures firsthand, and then bring some of their wisdom and teachings back to the States with me.

If you're black, you need to get information right now! We can't be fearful we don't know who we are anymore. Personally, I'm tired of wondering am I a black man from the South with felonies and without a college degree, who somehow beat the odds that were stacked against me? Or am I the descendant of kings and queens who has actually inherited my birthright, who has walked into the greatness that should have been expected of me all along.

The answer is I'm a descendant of those Balanta, Mandinka, and Mende kings and queens.

The Mende people have been known as fighters. It was Mendes who took over the *Amistad* during the passage from Africa and eventually earned their freedom.

The name Balanta comes from the term "those who resist." They were people who managed to resist colonization and have held on to their traditions.

The Mandinka are the descendants of the Mali Empire, which during the thirteenth century was the richest on earth. Its library at the University of Sankore had more than one million manuscripts.

The point is I'm supposed to be someone who fights against my oppression in America. I'm supposed to love books. Hell, I'm supposed to be rich. That's what's in my DNA.

Even with that knowledge, I'm still struggling to figure out just how much my American roots mean to me. For years, I would have said they are the foundation that all my success has been built on. That without them, I'd fall apart. I'd be nothing.

But these days, I'm not so sure.

Are my roots holding me down?

Or keeping me *tied* down?

Deeply Rooted

Make no mistake about it, my roots are firmly in the soil of Moncks Corner, South Carolina. That's where I was raised. It's where I had some of my best times. And a place where I learned some of my hardest lessons. For that reason, Moncks Corner will always be my heart.

I'm going to host a turkey drive for Thanksgiving every year in Moncks Corner. I'm always going to sponsor a back-to-school book-bag giveaway for the students. I'm completely committed to my Third Eye Awareness foundation providing mentorship for teenagers in the area. I absolutely owe the town those things.

Outside of charitable work, I also rely on the town for emotional stability. As I wrote in *Black Privilege*, I still go back from time to time just so I can sit on the porch of my grandmother's house. She's long gone, but when I sit in the southern silence (people up north don't know what true silence is), I can still feel her presence. I can tap into some of the strength that she possessed as a black woman in the South in the days of segregation. That strength, passed to me in those quiet moments, continues to sustain me.

In *Black Privilege* I wrote:

> *In order to get your equilibrium right, you must return to your core. If you can still physically go back, jump in the car or on a plane and get there ASAP. Lie in your old bed and reconnect with your old dreams. Sit on your front porch and remember how you felt as a young man or woman. If your relatives aren't around anymore, close your eyes and talk to your grandma, or your grandfather, or the auntie who raised you. Celebrate that the street you might live on now is nicer, but also embrace that dirt road you grew up on. Appreciate that all your power emanates from that dirt and that you wouldn't have it any*

other way. You'll probably shed a few tears, but they'll be empowering. Not painful.

I still believe that.

To a degree.

As I continue with therapy, I'm also realizing that I've attached a certain amount of anxiety to losing touch with my roots. I worry that if I don't keep going back to Moncks Corner, don't spend some time every year sitting on Grandmother's porch, or in my old bedroom, I'll somehow lose a vital part of who I am.

I'm not so sure that's true anymore. If anything, I've started to think that I've created unnecessary anxiety for myself by trying to be *too* attached to my roots.

The truth is, hanging out where you're from, after you've left for bigger things, can be stressful. You have a strong desire to "keep it real." You don't want folks to think you're too "big-time" to rub shoulders with them anymore. You want them to see that you're still the same old G.

The problem is not that you change, but the people around you do. If I go out to a bar or a club back home, especially with family, one of two things will always happen: either someone will want to buy me a drink or ask me to buy *them* a drink. If I don't accept the drink, I'm an asshole. If I don't buy everyone else a drink quickly enough (which I always do, by the way), then I'm an asshole. It can feel like when they see me they're on some, "Oh, this nigga thinks he's a star," shit and then they go out of their way to show that they don't give a fuck about me. I wanted to relax, but it felt like I was always being tested, always being watched. It was stressful.

It got to the point where I felt like I didn't have anything in common with them anymore. That's the loneliest feeling in the world. To go back home and feel like the connection is gone. The only time I feel a little comfortable is when I'm home on holidays. Not because they remind me of happy memories (we didn't celebrate holidays) but because that's when most of the other people who've found success in the larger world come home too. Those are who I feel the strongest connection to— people who were raised in Moncks Corner but left to achieve success like me.

To be fair, there are still a couple—and I mean a couple— of folks in Moncks Corner who I am comfortable hanging out with. There's my man SP, who used to hustle out on Highway 6. SP's a good dude who held me down when I got off the streets. When I was trying to throw parties and make a name for myself in radio, he'd always show love and gave me money for events. We also had very similar taste in music and would have great discussions about the latest happenings in hip-hop. SP left the streets behind a long time ago and today has made a good career for himself in construction, so I never get the sense that he is looking for anything from me, and, most important, he doesn't act strange. We still hang out and shoot the shit about hip-hop like we always did. Last year I got us tickets to the Alabama–South Carolina football game in Columbia and we had a great time driving to the game, arguing about how rappers of today stack up against the MCs of our era. We've always had a lot in common, so the conversation still flows as easily as it did when we were kids.

There's also my cousin Kinta, who runs my Third Eye Awareness nonprofit. We're still tight, but truthfully we're more likely to hang out outside of Moncks Corner. Sometimes Kinta will come along with us on family vacations or visit me in NYC. Every year he also throws a dope-ass house party during the holidays. It's always fun as fuck because nobody is acting *strange*. Again, the key word is "strange." When you achieve success it's almost like people are expecting you to act different, so they start acting different first as a defense mechanism. Get a grip on your insecurities and act regular, please!

Outside of those two, I can truthfully say there isn't really anyone else I'm checking for when I come home. A few years ago I would have been afraid to admit that to myself, let alone write it in a book. Today, I accept that it's my truth and I'm not running from it anymore. That doesn't mean I'm bigheaded. Or that I think I'm too good for the folks I grew up around. It just means that I've evolved and I'm comfortable with what I've become and if you going to act *strange*, then I don't want to be around you.

If anyone in Moncks Corner feels a way about me saying that I don't want to hang out when I come home, then consider this: my father has his own little club—down South we call them sugar shacks—in Moncks Corner. He doesn't even want to be in the business anymore because of the shady characters who come through. My father has told me that he's had to call the cops several times because folks are selling drugs outside under the tree in his yard. Why in the world would I put myself in that situation anymore? So I can say that I'm still "keeping it real"? I'm keeping it real all right—real far away from any nonsense that might land me in a compromising situation.

One of the absolute worst things black men are taught growing up is that we've got to keep it real. And most of the time "keeping it real" involves some type of criminal activity. It's a lie told by people who are jealous of our potential. People who are envious we might actually make it out of a situation they hate and can't get out of themselves. Anyone who tells you that you need to keep it real by coming back to the hood is actually fake as fuck. Any love they profess to have for you is hollow.

If your people really love you, if they ask you to stop by the hood and you say hell no, they won't get defensive. They will understand. That's why if the homies saw that you had a talent that might get you out of the hood, they'd tell you to make your move and never look back. Anyone who tells you, "Yo, you a lame if you come back and don't kick it with us," is a fraud themselves.

Only time you will see me back in the hood is when I'm giving back to the hood. Pulling up just to kick it is a waste of time. And I want to be clear, I don't mean the general community I come from. No, you will see me kicking it in Moncks Corner, Columbia, or Charleston all damn day. I'm talking about the *hood*, the *skreets*, up under the tree, whatever you want to call it. I'm not going to give myself an unwanted anxiety attack trying to keep it real for y'all. I have to keep it real with myself first and foremost.

When I was in the streets I could never understand why guys would want to come back to that lifestyle. I had homies who got scholarships to play football in college. In the hood, getting a sports scholarship is like getting one of Willy Wonka's golden tickets to the chocolate factory. It's a chance to create a whole new life for yourself. You get to go off to UCLA or Miami or Michigan and experience something different. You get to start a new journey on someone else's dime. What could be better than that?

I would think not much. But so many of those guys would head home as soon as the school year was over. They could have been working out at school, or getting paid from some cushy job a rich alumni set up for them. They could have been doing summer internships or just hanging out in their frat house, kicking it with sorority girls every night—the types of options that are often open to you when you have a Division I football scholarship.

So when I'd see them around town, I couldn't help but think, "Nigga, what are you doing here? Why are you getting high under a tree in Moncks Corner when you could be living your best life down in Miami?"

They never seemed to have a good answer. They'd grumble about how they were tired of having to depend on their parents for money. How it wasn't fair that the NCAA was making so much money off them but they never saw a dime.

They'd hang around town for a few months and then inevitably get caught up in the dope game, since there aren't many other ways to make money in Moncks Corner. When it was time to head back to school in the fall, a bunch of them never went back. They just hung out in Moncks Corner, selling drugs and getting high.

A couple of years later they'd look up and realize they'd pissed away their best opportunity for success. By then, of course, it was too late to get another scholarship. Too late to get noticed by the NFL. Too late to take advantages of the connections that come off the field from being a big-time college athlete. Instead, they'd opted to keep it real in Moncks Corner.

At the time I couldn't understand why they'd give up so easily, but today I can see a lot of it had to do with anxiety. I never went to college myself, but I'm sure it's very stressful to be from a small town like Moncks Corner and find yourself on a major college campus. Even if you're a D-I athlete. Your roommate might be from New York or Los Angeles. They might be knowledgeable about stuff you've never heard about.

They might dress better than you. Have more money than you. Know about foods you've never tasted. Try talking to a dude from NYC about hunting deer and then eating it. He will look at you confused and disgusted. Like you just told him construction Timbalands are *trash* . . .

My cousins might have been big dogs back in Moncks Corner, but on a college campus they probably felt like country bumpkins. Which made them insecure. Which made them sad.

What do most people do when they feel unsure of themselves in a new situation? They retreat back to the familiar. They return to what's comfortable. Even if it's not in their best interest.

This is why I feel the motivation behind "keeping it real" isn't really loyalty. It's not bravado. It's not fearlessness.

It's anxiety.

Once you can accept that, it becomes easier to get past it. It's OK to feel out of place in a new situation. There's no shame in not knowing about certain fashions, customs, or foods. That's the whole point of evolution. You take your core and then build on it. Not retreat back into a negative space.

To anyone who feels insecure about stepping out of the hood and into a better opportunity, I'd remind you of the old quote, "It's better to try and fail than fail to try." My cousins, and so many hood kids just like them around the country, failed to try. Don't make that same mistake.

And to be clear, not hanging out doesn't mean never giving back. No, you've always got to do that. But just by making it to a new place, you're showing the hood that evolution is possible. You're showing a path that people like you can take to help reach another level in life.

Once you get there, by all means give back to the community. Create a nonprofit. Help build some affordable housing. Offer kids scholarships. That's how you make a difference. But you don't have to go back if you don't want to. You don't have to sit on the same bench you sat on as a kid smoking weed. You don't have to stand around drinking and playing CeeLo on the same corner you used to. What are you proving by that? Only that you don't value your success.

Survivor's Remorse

I no longer feel the need to hang out when I'm in Moncks Corner, but I still feel a lot of anxiety about the people I've left "behind." Yes, the pettiness and jealousy I encountered can get under my skin, but at the end of the day I truly want all of them to experience the same success I have. I want their world to expand like mine has. I want their future to look as bright as mine does.

That's because I know the odds they've faced their whole lives. I know the dysfunction they've been embroiled in. I've felt the desperation that can hover over you like a cloud.

Sometimes I wonder: Why was I able to overcome the hurdles that tripped them up? Sometimes fatally.

Was it my father staying on my case all those years? Refusing, for all his own BS, to let me succumb to the streets?

Was it the influence of my mother? The schoolteacher who instilled a love of reading in me?

Was it the presence of mentors like Dr. Robert Evans of Never So Deep Records, who always pointed me in the right direction when I reached a crossroads?

Or was it God herself? Who somehow kept me on the righteous path even when I was doing my damnedest to go astray?

I don't know.

I'm far from alone in asking those questions. There are so many men and women from the hood who have elevated their lives but are still troubled by a nagging sense that somehow they don't deserve it. Or who feel that their success came at someone else's expense.

There's a term for this feeling: "survivor's guilt." It refers to the guilt someone can feel when they survive an event that has damaged, traumatized, or killed people around them.

It's an emotion people have probably been feeling for thousands of years, but therapists first put a name to it after working with Jews who had survived the Holocaust. Those survivors were haunted not only by the trauma they'd experienced but also by guilt. Some couldn't wrap their heads around being alive after having seen so many others die. Others felt guilty about what they had done to survive—maybe stealing food from another Jew at the concentration camp, or avoiding a situation that led to another Jew's death. They made hard choices in order to survive in captivity, but once they were free they had a hard time living with those decisions.

Survivor's guilt was also prevalent in the gay community following the AIDS crisis of the eighties and early nineties. So many people lost friends, family members, and lovers. Some questioned the fairness of a world where they were alive but their partners died. Others felt guilty for not doing enough to protect a friend, or a family member, from choices that would ultimately kill them. And many simply felt depression and rage over so little being done to fight a disease that killed so many bright and talented people.

Survivor's guilt has also been a major theme in hip-hop. Most rappers came from the hood, where they might have experienced poverty, racism, violence, and abuse. Once they get some real money in their pockets, they make the move to the suburbs to get away from all that dysfunction. Some folks call the towns of Fort Lee and Englewood in New Jersey "Rappers' Row" because so many rappers live there in luxury apartments overlooking Manhattan. But there's also a lot of pain that comes with leaving the hood behind. The memory of the homies who died before they got a chance to taste success with you. The knowledge that even though your circumstances have improved, there are so many other hardworking, good-hearted people who are going to stay stuck in the hood for the rest of their lives.

One artist who has done an incredible job at articulating survivor's guilt is Kendrick Lamar, especially in his classic album *To Pimp a Butterfly*. A native of Compton, Kendrick talks a lot about his difficulty reconciling his newfound fame with the lives most of his homies are still living back on the streets. He told MTV,

> You living this life . . . but you still have to face the realities of [what's happening back at home]. . . . I gotta get back off that tour bus and go to these funerals. It's definitely survivor's guilt. . . . How can I be a voice for all these people around the world and can't reach them like I want to? And they're the closest to me? That's a trip.

According to Kendrick, that sense of being unable to help elevate his homies almost drove him insane.

> That can draw a thin line, you know, between having your sanity and losing it. This is how artists deteriorate, if you

don't catch yourself. . . . My release, therapy, is writing the
music.

LeBron James is not a rapper, but another person whose words on survivor's guilt have resonated with me. He even produced a TV show called *Survivor's Remorse*, which is loosely based on his life. LeBron touches on the other side of the coin Kendrick discussed, which is the feeling that your homies are mad at you for leaving them behind. He told CNN,

> *I have always had a problem with people saying you've changed over the years. I would hope that you've changed— for the better. . . . My problem is I would always tell them, "You are the one with the issue, because you have not changed, you're still in the same position you were four or five years ago." And it happens in our society a lot. In the black community . . . we'd rather stay together and both struggle than one of us making it and us being happy for the person who made it.*

It's true. For too long there's been a crabs-in-a-barrel attitude in the hood. If we see someone getting "too big," our first instinct is to pull them back down to us. Instead of studying their moves so that we can get out too, we want to pull them back into the pack. You'll often hear people say, "Haters going to hate," as if it's a fact of life. I don't believe it always has to be this way though. I prefer to subscribe to the philosophy of "each one, teach one." That means if I get to a better place in life, I'm going to try to show you how to get there too. I'm going to put myself out there to help you, even if it gives you another chance to pull me back into the barrel. Or as the Queen Cardi

B famously said, "Don't be a 'why her and not me' type of bitch. Be a 'how can I get next to that bitch' type of bitch."

Of course, trying to help the homies back in the hood can create its own issue. I say there's a Jay-Z lyric for every situation, and trying to deal with survivor's guilt is no exception. In "Nickels and Dimes," he talks about the challenges of trying to live by the "each one, teach one" ethos. "Sometimes I feel survivor's guilt," he raps. "I gave some money to this guy, he got high as hell / Now I'm part of the problem far as I can tell."

I know so many other successful black folks have found themselves in this situation. Someone from your hood asks you for money and you feel compelled to say yes, even if you don't feel confident it's going to be put to good use. After all, this person is from the same place as you. You know what they've been through. What you've been through together. So you do them a favor, but they end up blowing the money and souring the relationship. Which leads to more tension and bad feelings. That's why in one of the next lines Jay raps, "I got a problem with the handouts / I took the man route / I'll give an opportunity though / That's the plan now."

Man, I am definitely on Jay's plan now. I'm not allowing guilt to cloud my judgment any longer. I'll lend a helping hand to anyone who needs it, but before I do, I need to see evidence that they're going to put it to good use. To give you an example, one of my homeboys texted me the other day asking for help getting his music "out there." That might sound like a fairly reasonable request, but to me it was ridiculous. This guy is closing in on forty and is still trying to get "put on" as a rapper. That drove me crazy, because if you're a student of the rap game in 2018, then you would know that no one gets "put on" anymore.

Thanks to the internet, you put yourself on now. You create some fire music and then build up a fan base online. You can record your music on a laptop if you can't afford studio time. You can film videos with your damn iPhone if you can't afford a videographer. If you're good enough, and consistent enough, over time you are going to get recognized. People are going to comment, follow you, like you, and retweet you. When that happens enough, *then* that's when a record label might be interested in you. If that record label doesn't come calling, you can still make some type of living from shows, streaming dollars, and merchandise if you're savvy enough. That's how you get on. Not because someone who's "made it" said you're hot. Those days are long over.

My friend should have known that, but he was hoping he could skip over all the steps that involved hard work. I had to set him straight. "Bro, stop asking me about music," I texted him. "You're almost forty. Let's find something else to work on together." I thought that was an honest, and encouraging, response. Maybe he'd hit me with a plan to open a fast-food franchise, or start his own construction firm. Those are the type of projects I want to support with my success. Not forty-year-old rap dreams.

My friend didn't see things that way. "Yo, man. Hit me when my friend come back," he quickly replied. "Because I don't know who this new nigga is."

"Yo, I'm the same person who's been telling you the truth your whole life," I texted back. "Just like I'm telling you the truth now. We both know you're not going to make it as a rapper. And that's not a diss. I love you to death. But you've got to figure out something else to do."

It's not easy to have a conversation like that with an old

friend, but it's necessary if you want to maintain a healthy relationship with the people you came up with. They might claim you've changed. That accusation will sting. But you've got to have the confidence to know that the issue isn't that you're different, but rather *they* have failed to evolve.

Yes, when I was nineteen, me and my homie were trying to make it as rappers, like a lot of other kids were. But at a certain point I took stock of my situation and accepted that I was garbage on the mic. How did I come to that realization? Because as my mentor, Dr. Robert Evans, was kind enough to tell me, "FUCK YOUR DREAMS, YOU SUCK AS A RAPPER." That forced me to admit that I didn't have what it takes. So I changed up my course and pursued a different avenue, which was radio. I was able to reach a much higher level of success in radio than I would have ever touched as a rapper.

My homie never took an honest stock of his situation. If you're still trying to "get on" more than twenty years after you started, either you're not good enough, disciplined enough, or passionate enough to make it as a rapper. You need to change course. Hell, you should *want* to change course. Who wants to keep driving down the same dead-end street year after year?

Unfortunately, some people do. They are just more comfortable staying stuck in that proverbial barrel than following their path to freedom. It can be very painful to be close to someone like that, but what I've learned is that you can't blame yourself for their inaction.

The only way you're going to be able to take care of the people around you is if you practice self-care first. That might sound selfish, but it's just common sense. Think about when you're about to take off on a plane and the flight attendants show you how to use the oxygen masks when they're released. What do they always say? If you're traveling with children, secure your mask first and *then* put on the child's. That's because they know you have to get your own situation secure before you can help someone else.

That's true in the rest of life too. You must make sure you've got your own situation together before you can truly help anyone else. It is OK to feel sad for your friends who seem to be stuck in place. Just as it's definitely OK to mourn for your friends or family who are no longer here. No one is saying that you can't feel that pain in your heart.

What you have to guard against, however, is being paralyzed by that guilt. When I recently told my mother I was feeling guilty about that conversation I had with my old friend—the one who said I'd changed—she cut me right off. "You don't have anything to feel guilty about," she told me. "You don't have to do things just because people ask. You didn't get to where you got by asking for things. You put in work, and good things happened. The people asking you for help can do that too. You don't owe them anything."

I went through something similar with a family member who had recently asked me for a loan. I've always made it clear that I'll be there for my family when there's a real emergency at hand. Sudden surgery, bail, funeral costs, I've got all of those. But I feel like too often I get hit up for situations that don't really merit me stepping in. Recently a family member had asked me to pay for their kid's summer camp. Of course I want the kid to go to camp and have a memorable experience, but I also know the kid's father has a good job. Why can't he pay for his own child's camp? I didn't know what to say, so I stalled in getting back to them with an answer.

Then one day I was looking at an Iron Man suit that I

wanted to buy for myself for Halloween. This thing was fully kitted out—body armor, handmade from fiberglass with flexible joints and LED lights in the hands, chest, and helmet. The Marvel fan in me just had to have it. The price tag, however, was three thousand dollars. I could afford it without a problem, but as I debated clicking the purchase button, I started feeling guilty. I was going to tell a family member I couldn't pay for one of their kids to go to camp, yet I was willing to pay three thousand dollars for a Halloween costume for myself? It didn't seem right. I was really conflicted, so I decided to ask my wife for advice. "Get the goddamn suit," she replied after I shared my guilt with her. "You work hard for your money. You don't owe anyone an explanation for what you want to buy for yourself. Plus, you're always helping people out. It's OK to say no!"

It was very freeing to hear that from my wife. Just as it had helped to hear something similar from my mother. My mother's message to me was the family has to stop asking for stuff unless it is an emergency.

I really appreciated my wife and my mother letting me know that it was OK to say no. Feeling that I owed people a yes was unnecessarily bringing anxiety and stress into my life. It was making me regret my hard-earned success, instead of enjoying it.

Which is not to mean that I've cut myself off from my roots forever. In discussing my mixed emotions with my therapist I realized that rather than worry about how other people feel, the most constructive thing I can do is focus my attention on the people who matter the most to me. I can work on making a difference in their lives.

I want to help the family of the people I feel like I owe. Those who are no longer here, like my brother Jerrell Garnett. We both grew up without having much. We both turned to selling drugs. We both had some talent. (Jerrell could rap his ass off. Much better than I ever could.) We spent a lot of time together dreaming about making it as rappers.

But even after I turned my attention to radio, Jerrell never fully removed himself from the streets. Eventually our paths diverged, even though we would speak all the time and see each other whenever I would go down to South Carolina. Then a few years ago he was murdered in a recording studio in Moncks Corner. When I got that call, I really didn't know how to process his loss. I was, like, damn, but I didn't cry. I didn't smash a window or fall to the floor in tears. I didn't even call his family to offer condolences. I just went numb. Emotionally, I turned a channel and didn't look back.

When it was time for his funeral, I sent some flowers and paid respects to his mother, Jimmy Sue, but that's all I could do. The guilt was killing me. It didn't seem fair that I got to enjoy life with my kids, but his would never have their father. I felt like I could have done more to get him out of the hood, but I wasn't quite in position yet to do that. Or maybe I was already in position and didn't realize it. If I had promoted his music more, promoted him more—then maybe he wouldn't have stayed on the streets. He'd be alive today. Those children would have a father. Jimmy Sue would still have her son, but then I'm like, well, he didn't die on the streets, he died in a recording studio working on his dreams, the bullets weren't even meant for him. . . .

I couldn't really articulate those emotions before going to therapy and writing this book. It was too tough. Too painful to consider. But now that I have, I realize avoiding that pain wasn't the answer, because it never really goes away. Instead, it just keeps me stuck in place emotionally.

To move forward, I really need to do something meaningful for Jerrell's kids. For his mother. It might be money, but it could just be opportunity. Maybe it's just stopping by and talking to his kids about their father. Right now I don't have a relationship with them at all. I can build with them about all the great times I had with their father and what a special, talented person he was. And when they're a bit older, I can maybe lend a hand to help them realize their dreams.

Hopefully they will read this and one day come to me with this page to hold me to my word!

Taking specific, impactful steps for the people you care about is the best way to deal with survivor's guilt. I can't worry about what a bitter old classmate in a bar might say about me, or whether an old friend is upset I won't bankroll his pipe dreams.

What I can do (and what anyone feeling survivor's guilt can do) is try to impact the lives of those I still feel the closest bond to. I can't "save" all of Moncks Corner, just like Kendrick can't save all of Compton, Jay-Z all of Brooklyn, or LeBron all of Akron. But we can direct resources to work wherever our heart tells us they'll have the most meaningful impact.

You can also make a difference by representing on the platforms you've built. If you know me, you're probably sick of me talking about Moncks Corner, or South Carolina. But there's a reason I do that. I need to let the people back there know I haven't forgotten about them. That they do matter. That's why you probably already know that Jay is from Brooklyn, LeBron is from Akron, and Kendrick is from Compton. We all appreciate what our hometowns have done for us. We're all committed to inspiring future generations.

Sometimes people ask me, "Being that you rep South Carolina so hard, does it bother you that your kids are going to grow up repping Jersey?" I have thought about it, but at the end of the day, if having my kids rep the South was that important to me, then that's where they would live. Do they have a connection to South Carolina? Absolutely. Do they love going down there to visit family? Without a doubt. But it's still foreign territory to them at the end of the day. They're going to be East Coasters, and that's cool.

Almost every city I go to—New York, LA, Chicago, Philly—I'll meet someone who will tell me, "Oh, I got family down South. I used to go down there for summers when I was a kid." That's who my kids are going to be when they grow up. City kids who have a connection to the South. And that's fine.

Still Ain't Forgave Myself

Sometimes I feel uncomfortable even talking about survivor's guilt because it makes me wonder, have I *really* survived the hood? Yes, I'm physically not there any longer, but will my past still catch up with me?

People who grew up in the streets don't tend to spend a lot of time thinking about the poor decisions we made. We're quick to chalk it up to "the game." As my man Prodigy said, "There's a war going on outside no man is safe from." When you're in combat, you don't get caught up worrying about collateral damage. My crew and I fancied ourselves soldiers. We were fighting in a war and weren't required to pray for repentance and forgiveness from a higher power for what we did.

I now understand that was a mistake. Needing to ask for forgiveness is one of the biggest issues I've confronted through therapy. Like most hood dudes, I've spent a lot of time talking about how the streets affected *me*. What I haven't given nearly enough thought to is the effect I had on *other people*. That's something I haven't wanted to confront.

I haven't wanted to consider the people who were shot at because of my crew. The people we jumped. We robbed. The families whose lives were impacted by the drugs they got from us. I haven't wanted to try to come to terms with that.

While I was writing this book, a young lady did an interview and claimed I had sexually assaulted her at a party in 2001. I didn't do it. Some people said she was resurfacing because I was a celebrity. At the end of the day, the "why" doesn't matter. She was impacted by what happened at the party. That's the bottom line. And I hadn't spent much time thinking about her pain. When I told the story of the party in *Black Privilege*, it had been from my perspective. I had wanted to illustrate how scared I had been by the allegations and how I didn't want to find myself in that situation again. I wanted to highlight the moment when I realized it was finally time to leave my "street" friends behind once and for all.

In retrospect, I had been thinking too much about how that night affected *my* life. I hadn't given much thought at all to how it had hurt her. Obviously her reappearance in my life made me look at the situation in a whole new light. What I saw wasn't pretty. I'd been extremely selfish in how I told that story. My only concern was how it had impacted me. Not how it had impacted a teenage girl.

When I realized how selfish I'd been, I started reexamining many more situations from that period of my life. I was abusive to my teachers. I disrespected elders in my community. To say nothing of the fact I used to sell crack! I impacted a lot of people's lives negatively just because I wanted more money in my pocket and thugs to respect me.

To make matters worse, I'd gotten in the habit of patting myself on the back because I "made it" out of the streets. Yes, I'd made it, but at what cost? I've evolved from that selfish, destructive young man, but does that absolve me of the damage I've done?

That's a question I've been grappling with a lot in therapy. Through those conversations, I find myself not only asking for the forgiveness of others but also for the ability to forgive myself. T.I., one of my seven favorite rappers of all time, has a song called, "Still Ain't Forgave Myself," which features the hook:

> All the mistakes made on this road to wealth . . .
> Ay, what I am today, I made myself
> But I still ain't forgave myself

I feel the exact same way T.I. does. I know if I don't seek true forgiveness for my past transgressions, my anxiety will always play tricks on me.

Industrituionalized

When it comes to reconciling where I've been and where I'm at now, another one of the anxieties I've learned to let go of is my fear of being "of the industry."

For those who didn't read *Black Privilege*, I'm referring to the advice Wendy Williams once gave me: "You're either of the people, or of the industry." By that, Wendy meant as you begin to gain popularity and access, you're going to have to make a fundamental choice. You're either going to prioritize your relationship with your audience, aka the people, which means asking artists hard questions during interviews and refusing to play music-business politics, or you're going to be of the industry, which means you're going to prioritize your relationships with the artists, managers, publicists, A&Rs, and advertisers. You'll play things safe and be willing to ask softball questions during interviews in order to keep the industry happy.

Wendy's philosophy was that once you're "of the industry," you lose your edge and your connection to your audience. That made a lot of sense to me, so for many years being "of the people" was a top priority. I'd decline invitations to parties and trips because they felt too "industry." If a rapper wanted to get dinner, I'd say no. If a producer wanted my opinion on a track, depending on who it was I had no problem pulling up and giving it to them. But that's where it stopped. I sent a clear signal to not try to offer me anything "out of the goodness of your heart," because my opinion could not be bought.

Industry people want you to accept a favor from them as they believe that once you have you will abide by the code to never say a negative word about them, which is complete bullshit. Don't get mad when I tell you your shit was wack or tell the world via radio your shit was wack. I wouldn't lie to my real friends, so why would I lie to you? That's what the old industry does—circle-jerk each other and lie to one another.

What I've learned over the last few years, however, is the "old" industry is dying fast.

I am of the "new industry."

And it's OK.

I've been part of the radio/TV industry for almost twenty years now. It's only natural that I'm going to gravitate toward, and build relationships with, people who do the same kind of work and share the same passions that I do. If anything, it would be unhealthy if I *wasn't* building those sorts of relationships.

I started in radio, but since then I've evolved. I've branched off into other industries like books, TV, film, and podcasts. As I've grown, I've watched other people who also started at the bottom (you can't get more bottom than getting fired from a radio station in Columbia, South Carolina) make similar strides in their own careers. People who started as interns, board ops, overnight hosts, and struggling rappers but who now are calling their own shots. People who I dreamed with. Plotted with. Broke bread with. Who shared my dreams and are now in positions of power through media and other forms of entertainment.

The other day I woke up and glanced at my call log from the day before. The names I saw shocked me: Lil Duval, Killer Mike, Kanye, Pete Davidson, Tip, Angela Rye, Tiffany Haddish, and Amanda Seales. Then I saw a group chat with Hovain (manager of the Lox and Wale), Rob Markman from Genius, Nessa Diab and TT Torrez of Hot 97 (I went to high school with TT), B.Dot from Rap Radar, and Kaz from the *Flagrant 2* podcast and Uninterrupted's *The Score*.

I looked back at my phone and said, "What I have become? I'm doing exactly what Wendy warned me about. I'm selling out the people for the industry!"

I started to panic. Not heeding your former mentor's advice is a great way to ruin your career. Was that what I was doing? Then I caught myself and said, "There's nothing to be ashamed of here. There's nothing to panic over. Instead, thank God you have these relationships with such talented and interesting people. BECAUSE WE ARE THE INDUSTRY NOW."

The reason I was able to catch myself and calm down was because I knew all those relationships were genuine. They weren't people I met over a line of coke at a penthouse party, or on a yacht in Saint Barts. I'd met many of these people over a decade ago, long before they had achieved the level of fame they have today. For instance, I met Killer Mike in Columbia, South Carolina, in 2003 when he was signed to Big Boi from Outkast's Purple Ribbon All-Stars label. We remain tight. I met Lil Duval in 2006 on Myspace and immediately started working on the *Hood State of the Union* videos and have been friends ever since. I met Tip in 2002 when he was in between his record deal with LaFace and Atlantic, and Amanda Seales and I used to do a TV show together on MTV called *Hip Hop POV* in 2012. After tapings I would drop her off to her crib in Harlem in my 2003 Escalade with more than 200K miles on it. I met Tiffany Haddish more than twelve years ago but we didn't really start communicating and bonding until late 2016. Now that's my homie! I love her. She'll come to the house for dinner and I can count on two hands how many people have been to my crib and met my kids. I met Pete Davidson when he was seventeen years old after a taping of MTV's *Guy Code* and he tagged along to a dinner with Duval and me. Since then Pete and I talk all the time. Our relationship is very deep. I've literally talked him off the ledge several times. I'm friends with his mother and his sister. I don't care if he's on *Saturday Night Live*. Pete's my guy.

My industry relationships are genuine, and the connections are real. It's a new industry that we rise in together!

I've also been fortunate to build relationships with some

really talented people who similarly came from South Carolina. Bakari Sellers, a former state representative and a CNN commentator, has been a friend for years. We connected because of our common South Carolina roots. It's the same with Chadwick Boseman. We linked up three or four years ago when we realized we were both from South Carolina. Today he's the Black Panther and one of the biggest movie stars in the world. I could have never predicted that. He's someone I call homie because he's from South Carolina like me. I've got a similar relationship with Stephen Colbert. He's also from South Carolina, and his brother was even my English teacher back in high school. You don't think we have some common ground? Of course we do. So why wouldn't we be friends?

From now on, I'm being friends with the people I feel a connection with and supporting the artists I feel deserve my support. Take my relationship with Cardi B. I've been supporting her since I first saw her on Instagram and thought she was funny, with a unique POV. Nobody was pushing her or offering me anything to cosign her. I just liked her. In fact, Cardi has said plenty of times herself, "Charlamagne believed in me when none of these other motherfuckers did."

Still, to hear social media tell it, I've been trying to cash in on her fame. I saw one guy post a picture of me with a platinum plaque Cardi's label Atlantic Records had sent me (mind you, almost everyone in the music industry, especially radio, gets plaques from labels). "See! Look at Charlamagne posing with that platinum record for 'Bodak Yellow,'" he wrote. "You know he's definitely getting a check from her!"

In the past I would have let a comment like that, no matter how ridiculous, get under my skin. I would have thought, "I wasn't getting paid, but maybe it looks like I am getting too close to the artist. I need to back up." I'm not worried about that nonsense anymore. I support Cardi because she's a talented artist who has remained 100 percent authentic through all the ups and downs. I think that's an important example for other girls coming up from the hood.

I think examples like Cardi's have made it easier to accept being "of the industry." That's because industry isn't the same as it once was. The world Wendy was describing is fading away. Someone like Cardi didn't follow a "traditional" path to become the hottest female rapper in the game. She didn't have to spend years pitching her demo to a major label, and then the label made her famous through its marketing campaigns. Instead, she created her own buzz, through social media, TV, and mixtapes. Then, when she had all the leverage, she signed a deal.

That's the difference between now and where things were ten or fifteen years ago. People like Cardi are taking their destinies in their own hands, creating their own lanes, and building their own fan bases. That means the people, and not the industry, are deciding who and what they fuck with. The industry can't rely on the same cookie-cutter formulas they used in the past. The labels, networks, and stations are being forced to accept and tolerate nontraditional energy and approaches. The result is that real, authentic people are getting opportunities they never received before. And when they do succeed, they're becoming the new "industry." That's why I can't feel bad about being of the industry anymore. Nope. No need to have anxiety over "selling out" because I'm not selling out. It's just now the industry is *buying in* to real. I'm part of a new movement, a new industry where nobody is a gatekeeper because there are no gates. We control the cool, and I represent a generation of hustlers who truly do it for the culture and not the "industry."

Dropping My Demons

While I always cherish my overall experiences in Moncks Corner, I did do plenty of things there that I'm not proud of today. I've sold drugs to my community. I've cheated on the woman I love. I was involved in a shooting that could have left someone dead.

One of the best things about therapy is that it gives you space to confront your demons. To take the shit you've been trying to hide in the back of your mind and finally hold it up to the light. Therapy allows you to take a clear look and examine it for what it is. This is necessary, because you're never going to make progress if you don't confront the things in your past that are still weighing you down emotionally.

In high school I had a situation with a beautiful young lady who we can call Tiki. She had been on and off with my cousin Evan throughout most of middle and high school. Then one summer she and Evan started going through it and Tiki began calling me for guidance. Like I told you earlier, people coming to me for guidance has been a reccurring theme in my life. Like I also said earlier, relationships between men and women that are built on advice often become physical. That was the case with us. I started off giving her advice, and soon I found myself giving her something else entirely.

And she opened my eyes to how good sex could be. If she'd call and tell me to come over, I'd sneak out my window, jump on my dirt bike, and pedal the five miles to her house without even thinking twice about it. I just couldn't get enough of her.

People who knew us, however, didn't approve of our relationship. People were saying, "How did y'all end up together?

Lenard and Evan are really good friends. Plus they're related."
It seemed foul to a lot of folks in town, almost like incest. It was
foul, but this girl had me so open I couldn't care less about what
people were saying.

Tiki absolutely blew away anyone I had ever been with before.
We'd be playing Jodeci, H-Town, Silk, all that fly shit that was
popping in the mid nineties, during our lovemaking sessions,
and she would just wear me out. I was wrapped around her finger, and she knew it.

I even went to the mall and bought her a heart-shaped gold
ring. I could barely afford it, but I wanted her to know how
much I loved her. Do you know this young girl had the audac-
ity to get the ring appraised? Who the hell gets a ring appraised
as a teenager? Tiki. That's who.

It must not have been appraised for much, because Tiki
started clowning me about how cheap that ring was. The problem was, Tiki had an older half sister, let's call her Lisa, who
was into dating guys with money, including a few drug dealers.
These guys were buying her real gold, nice clothes, and even
cars. Everything I did was being compared to them and there
was no way I could measure up. I became wildly insecure about
pleasing Tiki, which just made my efforts fall even shorter each
time. The harder I tried to impress her, the less interest Tiki
seemed to have in me. It got to the point where I was having
panic attacks because she wouldn't take my phone calls anymore or answer the door when I rang.

One of my attacks was so bad that my mother called my
father and had him come talk to me. When he found me, I was
babbling about how I loved Tiki and didn't understand why
she didn't want to be with me. As was his custom, my father
didn't pull any punches and got to the (unromantic) heart of

the matter. "You got your nose open over this girl and she out here fucking you and probably everybody else in a thirty-mile radius," he scolded me.

I realize now that he would probably have said that about any girl making me crazy, but hearing it then instantly calmed me down. My cousins had been telling me she was no good for me since Tiki and I first got together, but I chalked it up to them being haters. They were just jealous because I had Tiki and they didn't. I had to accept what my father was telling me was the truth.

Once I regained my sense, I stopped sweating her. Stopped being so clingy. I fell completely back and didn't call her or try to see her. Within forty-eight hours she called me up and wanted to know where I'd been. I managed to play it cool for a few days and act like I wasn't interested anymore, but eventually we had sex again and I immediately went right back to being completely sprung.

One night Tiki and I were hanging out in my mom's house. My mom had a policy where I had to keep my door open, so Tiki and I devised a little routine by which we could slyly have sex. I'd stand up against the wall next to the open door and pull out my little meat. Tiki would stand in front of me, pull her shorts to the side and I'd get a couple of pumps in with my mother none the wiser.

I guess Tiki got bored with our little game because after a while she announced she was going to go hang out with Lisa. I didn't want her to go, even begged for her to stay, but Tiki wasn't trying to hear it and took off to go see Lisa.

All I could do the rest of the night was lie in bed and obsess over the idea that Tiki was out there running around with all the older drug dealers Lisa was down with. Guys who had their own apartments and could afford hotel rooms. It was driving me insane.

Finally I did what all people who suffer from anxiety do at one in the morning when they can't sleep: I went out for a walk. It just so happened that Lisa only lived a short ways down my dirt road, so I headed over there to see what I might find. It wasn't a long walk, but it added to my anxiety, because when you're out in the country at that time of night all you can hear is the loud drone of insects and unidentified animals howling in the woods.

I got to Lisa's right at the same time her car pulled up to their driveway. They must have seen me lurking in the shadows, because Tiki hopped out and said, "What the hell are you doing out there?"

"Slangin'" I stupidly replied. It was stupid because I wasn't doing that yet. Tiki let out a huff at my foolishness and went back to the car, at which point I noticed an older dude, probably around twenty-five, sitting in the back seat.

"Who's that?" I demanded.

"Oh, that's just our cousin," Tiki replied.

Right about then I noticed that Tiki smelled like sex. (What does sex smell like, you ask? The perfect mixture of a SoulCycle class and a cake store). "You smell like you were fucking," I told her.

"Yeah, because you and me had sex tonight," she replied, and then went into the house with her sister and her sister's "cousin."

There was nothing to do but go home, but in my mind something wasn't right. There was no way our little stand-up sex had left her smelling like that. I became convinced that Tiki was sleeping with Lisa's "cousin."

Because I had no confidence in myself, I couldn't let it go. Over the next couple of days I kept brooding over what Tiki must be up to. Finally I couldn't take it anymore and decided to take a walk over to the cousin's house, which also wasn't too far from my mom's house.

When I got to his yard, it sounded like someone was blasting a porno over club speakers. There was no denying it, I could clearly hear Tiki's voice screaming a name in ecstasy from inside the house. A name that very clearly wasn't mine.

Standing outside this older guy's house and listening to him Wu-Tang torture my girl's womb, suddenly all my fears, all my insecurities, and all my paranoia hit me at once. For a brief moment I thought about killing myself. If I'd had a gun on me, I probably would have. Thankfully I didn't.

I also didn't have any weed or liquor to help numb the pain, so I just stumbled out of his yard and sat down on the side of the dirt road. Where I proceeded to cry my eyes out.

At that point one of my homeboys, let's call him Bunz, happened to come down the street and saw me sitting there in tears. He just shook his head and said, "It's Tiki, ain't it?"

I said yes, and then explained what I just had heard.

"She's getting fucked right now?" he asked. "Man, let's go listen."

For some reason I agreed to return to the scene of the crime, but we had barely approached his house before we heard Tiki screaming.

"Whoooa, he fucking the shit outta her!" exclaimed Bunz. That pretty much put my insecurity through the roof. To his credit, Bunz stayed with me and tried to help me see the big picture. "Women are like buses. If you miss one, in the next ten minutes another one coming." That helped me calm down a bit and I agreed it was time to let Tiki go once and for all.

My plan worked for three days, until Tiki called and invited herself over to my mom's home. All my resolution to leave Tiki alone melted in a matter of seconds. While I waited for her to show up, my mind began racing over why she was actually coming to see me. "Does this mean she does love me?" I asked myself. Then I started thinking that maybe it meant that the older dude wasn't properly dicking her down (as if my ears had been deceiving me). "Man, if I can blow her back out today, she'll probably stick with me for good," I told myself. "This is my chance. I gotta really put it down." By the time Tiki showed up, I was a nervous wreck.

I wasn't sure what was going to happen, but we immediately got down to the business of having sex. Sadly, instead of blowing out her back, I let the pressure get to me. I performed more like the guys Missy Elliott was talking about in "One Minute Man." Hell, I probably didn't even last that long. I'm talking I got maybe five or six pumps and it was over.

When Tiki realized what had happened, she was downright disgusted. She pushed me off her and starting yelling, "See, that's why I'm fucking [older dude's name] now!"

When Tiki said that, I'd never felt so sorry in my life. All I could see was white light. My heart started beating so hard in my chest that I could hear it. I felt a knot grow in my throat, and I became extremely angry. Now I don't condone ever getting physical with a woman, but when she kicked my already severely bruised ego by making fun of my premature ejaculation, the truth is I snapped. I could barely see straight, and mushed her with my elbows.

I was in a rage for about ten seconds before I snapped out of it and realized I'd fucked up. Badly. I hadn't used my hands, but it didn't matter. I'd gone out like a sucker. I immediately tried apologizing to Tiki, but she wasn't trying to hear it. Instead, she started tearing down pictures I had of her up on my wall and ripping them to shreds. Every time I got near her to try to get her to stop, she'd start swinging at me. Eventually a friend of ours came and picked her up to take her home.

Tiki told her mother, the OG Gretchen, what I did. Gretchen rightfully was upset and called me on the phone. "I'm so disappointed in you," she told me. "I would never think you would do something like this."

I didn't have a good answer for her.

Remember when I said there was a period when I kept getting in fights and couldn't defend myself? Those incidents all took place right after my phone call with Gretchen. At the time, I attributed them to not being able to defend myself to the roots Gretchen must have put on me for what I did to her daughter. In fact, up until very recently I believed that all those beatings I took were because Gretchen had essentially cast a spell over me.

It wasn't until I started going to therapy that I was able to grapple with this incident and start to understand that my actions (or lack thereof) during that period had nothing to with Gretchen and everything to do with my inability to come to terms with what had happened with Tiki.

Tiki and I still kicked it for a while after that, but for decades I had been carrying around this delusion that somehow she had wronged me by cheating on me with an older dude. That she had been responsible for my anxiety attacks while we were together and indirectly responsible for what happened afterward.

Another thing I got wrong was partly blaming her for selling drugs. It was after my relationship with Tiki imploded that I started my relationship with the streets. In my mind, if I had just had the trappings of a drug dealer—the nice cars, the real gold, my own apartment—then maybe Tiki would have been more into me. I can't say that I started dealing drugs because of her, but I did feel a need to prove myself after losing her to that older dude.

I can now see, however, that all I had really done is trade one bad relationship for another. In the end, dealing drugs didn't leave me any more fulfilled, and it would prove just as damaging.

What my therapist has helped me see is that while I can't go back and undo what happened with Tiki, I can learn from it. What I can learn from it is I have to have the strength to detach from toxic relationships once I realize I'm not happy with where things are going. Obviously I'm not dating anymore, but there are other relationships, both professional and personal, that still feel harmful to me. I have to let go of those.

The first step in doing that is to put the responsibility on myself. For years and years I had blamed Tiki for what happened. She'd manipulated me. She'd forced me to lose my mind. I can now see that's just weakness on my part. Tiki was just a kid, who herself was getting manipulated by that older guy. The truth is I had an extremely fragile ego. I talked tough, but my confidence was brittle. I was very insecure and couldn't handle being with someone who seemed so much more mature than me.

My therapist has also led me to understand that in order to fully move on from a toxic relationship, I need to have closure. You can't just drift away from it, there has to be a moment where you and the other person know it's over.

In this case, I had always felt I'd achieved that, though I hadn't known what to call it at the time. While I eventually lost touch with Tiki, I did stay close to her mother, Gretchen. I made sure to visit and call Gretchen as much as I could, because I really respected her. During one of our last conversations before she passed from a long illness, she told me, "You know, Lenard, you're a good person. You just have to learn some lessons." When she said that, it felt like a weight had been lifted off my shoulders. It didn't absolve me from what I'd done, but I felt better knowing I had Gretchen's forgiveness. I vowed to never make the same mistake again and have lived up to it.

Fear of Losing My Roots and Dropping My Demons
Clinical Correlation
by Dr. Ish

One of the things we teach in therapy is the difference between your "public self" and your "private self." That is, the difference between the way you see yourself and the way you think other people see you. Oftentimes there is a huge gap between the two. Trying to reconcile the difference between the two sides of this coin can feel like an uphill battle that you're always losing. And you will lose this battle every single time until you finally realize it's not a battle you actually have to fight. Because the truth is you will never be able to control what someone else thinks of you. It's hard enough to control our own minds, much less everyone else's. The key is to control what you can, and that's only yourself. Specifically how you feel about yourself. How you see yourself. How close you feel you are to living your most authentic life on a moment-to-moment basis. Once you satisfy the balance of that equation you'll never have to worry about satisfying what everyone else thinks of you because you will have wrapped yourself firmly in the knowledge of self that keeps you focused on your purpose as you move through the world. When you know who you are you never have to worry about how to act or what to do in any situation; you can just relax and be you.

A huge take-home lesson from this chapter is the idea of "survivor's guilt," which is a very common theme in the black community that has to do with the concept of coming from humble beginnings and going on to becoming successful. And specifically concerning the feelings you have about those family members and friends you knew who didn't. There's guilt about surviving, guilt about what you "should" have done, and guilt about what you had to do to get out, particularly whom you had to leave behind. There's an old saying we hold near and dear to our hearts in the African-American community and that's "If you forget where you're from, you're never going to make it where you're going." It's empowering and limiting all at the same time. Remember, two things can be true. The truth is that you should never be ashamed of where you're from or who you're from. The trick is to stop telling that story from a victim's perspective and tell that story from a place of power, in which you can show all the

177

obstacles you had to overcome to make it and let every-one know that if not for the love and tough lessons you learned back then, you wouldn't be the person you are today. Learn to retell your story triumphantly. The other truth to this statement that holds people back is that they make a false assumption in thinking this means you can never turn the page on the person you used to be without turning away from the people too. That's simply not true. Oscar Wilde wrote, "The aim of life is self-development. To realize one's nature perfectly—that is what each of us is here for." You absolve yourself of the survivor's remorse by reminding yourself of this idea and using that to refo-cus you on your purpose every day. You absolve yourself of the guilt by remembering the people who struggled and sacrificed for you to have a chance to make it and honor them by living your best life. You absolve yourself of the guilt by realizing that the best way to save people is not by rubbing salve on their ego wounds by rejoining the fold, it's by blazing the trail and being the living exam-ple of how they can follow the steps you took to get sim-ilar results on their path. Your job is to lead first, then give back. The Sankofa bird is a mythical bird of West African (specifically Ghana) origin. The word translates to "go back and get it." It's represented as a bird that flies forward while looking backward with an egg, which sym-bolizes the future, in its mouth. Understanding your past informs your present and ensures your future. Your job is to be that bird.

From working with people from all walks of life I've learned that the secret to happiness and sustained suc-cess isn't the achievement of a specific goal. Happiness isn't a result; it's a choice. Happiness is being able to enjoy the person you're becoming all along the way. Life is about growth. Life is about learning. Life is about evolving into the person you were put here to become. It's impossible to do that while trying to stay the same. You're not here to be stagnant water. You're here to flow in whatever direction the current of your purpose pulls you.

The critical moment in any doctor-client therapeutic relationship comes when we look to see if you'll be able do what we refer to as "heeding the call to normalcy." Sadly, everybody isn't able. But for those who can, you'll find that the biggest hurdle to doing so isn't making up for what you don't have or overcoming what you've been through or gathering the tools you need to take the next step forward; the biggest hurdle to living the life that was truly meant for you is simply giving yourself permission to do so. It's OK. You're worth it!

Being in love with another person is hard. Learning how to be in love with ourselves is even harder. And nothing cuts quite so deep as the rejection associated with a first love; that's the worst. Charlamagne asks the one question that everyone who's ever had a heartbreak asks, "Why?" Ask a terrible question, your brain has no choice but to give you a terrible answer; which in this case was "Because who you are isn't enough for her." And from there things go completely off the rails. Rejection triggers uncertainty and insecurity inside us. Rejection helps us to believe that the worst we think about ourselves may actually be true. Once that message lands and your deepest, darkest thoughts are confirmed, it makes you feel a certain type of way. Anxious, embarrassed, ashamed, defeated, guilty, frustrated, angry, and ultimately, enraged.

Think. Feel. Do. We think a thought. We feel a corresponding emotion. We take a consequent action. There's no rage more dangerous than that of a teenager who hasn't yet learned the critical life skill of impulse control and feels justified in taking action, however poorly thought out and violent it may be. Bad things happen. Things that at their most unfortunate, can change the course of a young life forever. As a man with five sisters and eight aunts whom I love dearly let me be absolutely crystal clear: hitting a woman is wrong. Putting your hands on a woman in frustration or anger is wrong. Physically intimidating a woman for any reason is wrong. Doing anything to make someone feel less than is just wrong. I don't care what she said, what she did, or what she promised to do; hitting a woman is *never* an option. Charlamagne knew he had done wrong the second after it happened, but when you're hurt and angry the only thing you want to do is protect yourself and hurt back. People who are hurt, hurt other people. It's up to you to recognize that about yourself, take responsibility for your part in it, hold yourself accountable, and stop the cycle.

Which is what he ultimately did. There are three things you need to get over any big hurt: understanding, forgiveness, and closure. Super simple concepts to grasp but exceedingly difficult things to obtain. Charlamagne understood it was the realization of his own insecurity that fueled his rage and poured more gasoline on his anxiety bonfire. Anxiety is at its height when the things you think about yourself and feel about yourself and do with yourself don't match. In this situation his actions didn't match what he knew about himself deep down and it caused an explosion of emotion. All has to be in order for your life to feel in order. In his attempt to put those things back in line he sought forgiveness from the young woman's mother and was grateful to receive it. Ultimately, once you're able to forgive yourself and make the corresponding changes to make sure that never happens again in your life or the lives of those people you're lucky enough to affect, that leads to closure. This is how you heal.

We all make mistakes. We've all hurt someone either intentionally or unintentionally in the past. Understand it. Seek forgiveness, and if it's not available from them, give it to yourself. Close the loop. Move on with your life and do everything you can to make sure it doesn't happen in the lives of anyone close to you. We repeat what we can't repair. The cycle of anxiety, anger, and explosions is all too familiar in our community for a myriad of reasons and trust me; it's not a cycle that will serve you or anyone in your family well. Charlamagne was able to break his cycle. It's up to all of us to follow his lead and press pause on our own pathological patterns long enough to make a change.

CHAPTER 6

Parental Paranoia

"My daughter Zahra has asthma and spent a night in the hospital. I had no idea I could be scared like that. I was always one to just go, 'Ah I'm not dying or anything!' Until you have a kid you would give your life for, you have no idea that all of this is in you."

—Chris Rock

Every parent worries about their kids. It comes with the territory of being a parent. From stressing about the possibility of their toddler bumping their head on a playground set to freaking out when they go off to college, parents spend an incredible amount of time worrying about the possible dangers that may be lurking just around the corner.

Out of all the anxieties we can suffer from, parental paranoia is the one that probably makes the most sense. Our fundamental job as a parent is to keep our kids safe. As I've said, my parental business card might as well read, "Protect and provide." When we fear for our kids, or try to steer them away from potential threats, we're just being good protectors. It's in our DNA.

If we're judging by that standard, I'm a *great* parent. And

I mean world-class. I constantly worry about my kids' safety. I'm scared of everything. Of them getting kidnapped. Bitten by ticks that carry Lyme disease. Shortchanged by racist teachers. Attacked by terrorists. Trapped in school shootings. Bullied online. Being hit on by horny high school boys.

The list goes on and on. And I'm going to explore a lot of it, but one of the things I've been really digging into is the connection between being a good father and being a good husband too. More than ticks, terrorists, or teenage boys, what keeps me up at night is not making the same mistakes my father did.

Daddy Dearest

Before I get into my issues about my father—and I have plenty of them—I need to start by saying this: my father was *always* there for me. Despite everything that happened, I will *always* love him for that.

My father was a strong presence in my life. He always tried to teach me right from wrong, even if he sometimes had trouble making the right choice himself. He always pushed me. Prodded me. Punished me. Even occasionally praised me.

There are a lot—and I mean a lot—of men out there who went to sleep at night praying to have a father like mine.

But one of the things I'm learning from therapy is that despite the undeniable positive impact my father had on my life, he really messed me up in a lot of ways too.

And a good deal of it stems from how he treated my mother.

The stereotype for African-American men is that they are abandoned by their father at some point and are raised by a single mother. While this may be true for some, it was not my experience.

I was raised in a very traditional family structure. My father was always around and most definitely the head of the household. We might have lived in a trailer on a dirt road instead of a brownstone in Brooklyn, but in many ways my family resembled the Huxtables. Maybe not economically, but most definitely structurally.

When I watched *The Cosby Show*, it reminded me of my family and most of the families I knew growing up. Families that were intact. I'm talking about a husband, a wife, kids, and often grandparents, all under one roof. Next door to us were the Gibbses. They were a nuclear family living in what I considered to be a really nice house (it had a brick exterior and kitchen with a table where everyone could sit). Down the street were the Wilsons, who had a smaller house but the same family setup. Across from them were the Trotters, the Crowders, and also the Presidents. All those houses had fathers in them. That was just normal for us. On the other side of town, my wife was growing up the same way. Her parents are still together, and most of her friends grew up in similar households.

Looking back, the only friend I knew growing up who didn't have a father was my first white friend, Thomas. To be fair, we thought he had a father, who we called Jimbo. But just a few years ago I learned that Jimbo was actually Thomas's uncle. He was his daddy's little brother. Some real country shit.

The only time my father wasn't around in my childhood was when he had a court-ordered stay in rehab. In my mind, that didn't count as "leaving" the family. The state forced him to. So that wasn't on him. Today I might question some of the choices that led him into rehab in the first place, but back then I wasn't thinking like that. Hell, I didn't even know he was in rehab. I just knew he was gone and my mom took me to see him once that I can remember.

Things were good until I was a teenager. Then the incidents started. My mother would intercept or overhear phone calls that were always followed by arguments in our kitchen. I could feel a frostiness begin to settle over our trailer. I remember one time in particular where my father had been gone for a while and when he finally came back he had a new haircut. My mom flipped out on him, and when he tried to make a phone call, they tussled over the phone a little bit. I was fake asleep the whole time.

Then one night I was with my mother at Food Lion (a Southern grocery chain) and we saw a woman I didn't know wearing a Troop jacket that looked a lot like my father's. No one said anything to me, but I was starting to figure out what was going on.

One day, my father stopped coming home. Just like that. At first, he'd be gone for a few days at a time, then his absences became longer. A week. Then a few weeks.

After an attempt at a reconciliation, he was gone for a month. And then another.

And then when the months started to add up, I knew he wasn't coming back home.

Period.

Eventually, my parents got a divorce. The reasons why were never discussed with me, but I knew. He was a serial cheater, whether it was the woman in the jacket or the woman he would eventually marry. He ended up with a whole family completely separate from ours.

In my mind his decision wrecked our home. I believed that once he was gone, my mother had too much to deal with raising kids on her own. What little energy she had was directed toward my younger brothers and sisters. I started flying under the radar, receiving less supervision and getting into more and more trouble. My mother was trying to fix a broken heart and probably didn't have the strength to reel in kids. Not saying my little brothers and sisters were out of control, but raising kids is tough enough when you don't have to go through all the drama that my mom did.

I think my younger siblings suffered. My father had been there during the formative years of my older sister and me. His authority had been *strong*. My younger brothers and sisters never got that. My dad was way looser with them than he was with us. He was more of a friend to them than a disciplinarian. They struggled without that commanding presence in their lives, and I feel that absence has affected them to this day.

Despite its indelible impact on our family, my father and I never had an in-depth conversation about what happened. The closest we came to a discussion was when I was around nineteen. We were sitting in my bedroom, before he left for good. Out of the blue, I blurted out, "You're cheating on Mom! You got a whole other life, with a whole other family, going on right up the street!" I was almost crying. My father wasn't moved. He looked me dead in my eyes and simply said, "Right now you might only have one girl, but that's going to change. One day you'll understand." And guess what, there was a day when I *thought* I did understand. But today I don't.

What I don't understand today is why he never talked with me about what happened. Because we damn sure talked about everything else. We talked about crackas, the Dallas Cowboys, politics, James Brown, business, Minister Farrakhan, women, even the right way to sell crack. (Crackheads used to

187

call my mom's house and my father told me, "If you can't handle business better than this, you've got to get the fuck out of this house!") *Nothing* was off-limits. But for some reason he couldn't tell me why he'd left us. Let alone say "I'm sorry." I never heard those words from him.

When I was a grown man, he did tell me leaving my mother was his biggest regret in life. Maybe that was intended to give me closure, but it wound up making things worse. If he was truly content with his new wife, then at least I could have rationalized, "Hey, the two of them were just meant to be together." But when he said he regretted leaving my mother, that told me that he wasn't happy. He'd thrown it all away—the happy house, the loving children—for a mistake.

Discussing what he did with my therapist helped me see how much I've resented him. I hadn't realized how angry I had been with him over what he did to our family. Other things he did didn't bother me, and he's a wild boy. In 2011 I took him with me to MetLife Stadium to see the Jets play his beloved Cowboys. It was the tenth anniversary of 9/11 and some marines in our row took offense when he didn't stand for the national anthem. My dad has practiced both Islam and Jehovah's Witness, so he doesn't pledge allegiance, but the marines didn't know that. Words were exchanged. Then the marines wouldn't let my father leave his row to use the bathroom. "If you can't stand up for the anthem, we won't stand up for you now!" they told him. My father took that as a threat. So he tased them with a stun gun he always carried on his hip. (After this incident they changed the laws on what you could bring into a stadium.) All hell broke loose and my father ended up being arrested. Someone videotaped it and the incident was widely covered in the New York news.

Was I upset that I'd called in a favor to get him good seats and he'd repaid me by creating a spectacle? Not really. He has a right to sit during the national anthem as well as a right to defend himself. I pretty much shrugged the whole episode off.

But I could never shrug off what he did to our family.

I didn't grasp how hurt I truly was until I started discussing it in therapy. Not too long after I started therapy he left me a message saying he needed financial assistance to build a house in Moncks Corner. My initial reaction was, "Of course I'll help him. I owe my father that." I'd certainly given loans to people who weren't family before. Why wouldn't I help out my own dad?

But the more I thought about it, the more anxious I became about the ramification of a loan. I thought about who would live in that house I was paying for: the woman he'd left my mother for, plus her children and grandchildren. That was a sore point with me. My father, by his own choosing, barely had a relationship with my kids up until now. I think he's seen my eldest daughter once or twice in her entire life. Now I'm going to help pay for a house for his wife and his *other* grandchildren?

That lack of a relationship is a source of a lot of pain for me. One of the few times my oldest daughter saw my father was when he stopped by my mother's house over the holidays. My daughter and niece where both there, and after he left, my daughter told someone, "My cousin's grandfather was here before." What? I had to immediately tell her, "That man is your grandfather too!" My daughter had no clue. It hurt my heart.

Absentee grandfather or not, I still felt guilty about not lending him the money. I decided to ask my mother for advice. "Do you think it's OK if I just give him some of it and say, 'Yo man, here's a start. Go do what you gotta do'?" I wanted a solution that wouldn't leave me feeling so conflicted. My mother said there was nothing to feel conflicted about. "You don't owe him anything," she replied. "Don't feel guilty about saying no."

For a long time I kept putting off having the conversation with my father. I wanted to tell him that I couldn't help him until we'd addressed the issues between us. Thankfully, with a little coaxing from my therapist, I finally stopped being scared and had the conversation. Despite all the apprehension I'd built up in my mind, there was no pushback from him at all. He knew it wasn't right that he doesn't have a relationship with his biological grandkids. He accepted what I was telling him and actually said he was glad I'd confronted him. It was a real student-becoming-the-teacher moment. That's the beauty of life and the beauty of men being able to have grown-men conversations. I have no problem doing anything for him now that I got that off my chest, I'm a hold him down the way a son should as long as he holds down his grandkids the way a grandfather should. My only regret now is I didn't have that conversation with him sooner.

Recently my mother got her passport and I've started taking her to see different parts of the world. She absolutely loves these trips. I'd like to do the same thing with my father. Take him to the Caribbean. Even better, the motherland. I just got my DNA testing back from AfricanAncestry.com and found out that I'm 97 percent West African. Specifically, on my mother's side I'm descended from the Balanta, Mandinka, and Mende tribes located in the countries of Guinea-Bissau, Senegal, and Sierra Leone. My father's genetics are tied to the Balanta people living in Guinea-Bissau. It would be absolutely incredible to take my father with me back to Guinea-Bissau, to see exactly where we came from and walk among our true people. I have to imagine doing that with him would be one of the highlights of both our lives. But the thought also fills me with anxiety. If I buy him a ticket, I'd have to buy his wife one too. I simply couldn't do that to my mother. So if I do end up going, it won't be with him. And that emotionally fucks me up.

These are the types of issues I've been carrying around for too long that I finally get to unpack through therapy. I'm learning that's it's not healthy to keep all this turmoil and conflicted emotion inside. Especially when it involves family. I have to find a way to communicate my issues. Over the years, I've become very coldhearted about some things. I'll hear something hurtful, or upsetting, but I'll refuse to address it head-on. I'll tell myself, "I've got to keep moving," and try to get away from the hurt as quickly as possible. The result is that I've been living aspects of my life in almost a delusional state. I've been avoiding the reality of certain areas of my life.

Since I've started therapy, I've learned there is a psychological term for this called "compartmentalization." Basically, it's describes some people's ability to block out or not think about certain things that might get in the way of their goals.

Compartmentalization

Used correctly, compartmentalization can be an incredibly effective tool. If you're an entrepreneur, compartmentalization allows you to focus on what you need to do to succeed instead of worrying about the moves your competitors are making. If you're a wide receiver in the NFL, compartmentalization allows you to stay focused on making the catch when the ball is thrown to you, instead of freaking out that some linebacker is going to spear you and break your neck. If you're a working parent, compartmentalization allows you to leave your job behind at the end of the day and focus on your kids when you walk in the door from work.

Personally, I've always been very adept at compartmentalizing things, even if I didn't know I was doing it. It's how I was eventually able to get off the streets. I took all the negative energy the streets were sending my way and blocked it off in my mind. I could feel people trying to lure me back, but I refused to let those voices impact me. It's also why I didn't give up when I was fired from the radio four times. I tucked away all the discouragement and hate I got from those program directors in a little box in the back of my mind and stayed laser-focused on getting a new spot on the air.

The problem with compartmentalization is that while it can be very effective for your professional life, over time it can wreck havoc in your personal life. While it's OK, even necessary at times, to wall off emotions that feel like they're going to slow you down, at some point you need to address them. Otherwise, they're just going to sit in that little box you've created for them and start to sprout emotional mold. You might not feel it at first, but over time that mold is going to keep growing until it becomes extremely toxic to your well-being. Just like an old attic or garage that gets filled up with clutter, every once in a while you've got to open up your emotions and unpack all that stuff you've been hoarding away. Trust me, just like it feels great when you throw away all the junk from you house, it'll feel just as good when you get rid of the junk you've been hoarding in your mind.

I let way too much junk build up when it came to my relationship with my father. The pain he caused by leaving our family was too difficult for me to deal with, so I walled off all that resentment and anger toward him in my mind. For years I never addressed what I was feeling toward him. Even as my life was getting better and better I still couldn't figure out a way to slow down and finally address my issues with him.

Therapy has helped me understand that I need to break down those walls and air out my grievances. Otherwise that pain is always going to be holding me back, even if I'm not aware of it.

The situation with my father has been the most dysfunctional relationship in my life for many years. And he didn't even know it! I'm so glad I finally called to let him know how I felt.

I Let God Down

Despite all my anger toward and disappointment with my father, I spent a good part of my life following in his flawed footsteps.

I saw how much pain his cheating created, and how much he claimed to now regret it, but I still found myself making the same kind of mistakes. I wanted to walk with God when it came to my relationships, but I found myself dancing with the devil instead. It almost cost me dearly. As dearly as it cost my father.

My wife, Mook Mook, and I first got together in 1998 when we were both in high school. We had a good relationship, but I was young and immature and cheated on her. We broke up, then got back together before she went off to college. We decided to try a long-distance relationship, but like a lot of young women,

Mook Mook realized she needed to go through a hoe phase in college. Being the respectable individual that she is, rather than keep me in the dark and just cheat on me, she did the honorable thing and broke up with me.

Being the knucklehead that I was, I didn't want to hear it. I tried to argue with her and say she was only sleeping with dudes to get back at me. "Just because I was an idiot and cheated doesn't mean you have to do the same thing!" I tried to reason. "Y'all know men are dumb! No need to be as dumb as us!"

Unsurprisingly, that argument didn't get me anywhere. Mook Mook was having fun because she wanted to, not because she was trying to punish me. So after many unsuccessful pleading phone calls and letters (yes, we actually wrote physical letters back then), I resigned myself to having lost Mook Mook. It was a tough pill to swallow, because I knew she was special. I knew I wanted to spend the rest of my life with her. But I also knew that in order to have a shot at doing that, I needed to get my head right first.

I made a pact with myself: I was going to be a better man physically, mentally, emotionally, and, most important, spiritually. I was working at Hot 103.9 in Columbia at the time, and I began attending church on Sundays. OK, maybe not every Sunday, but I would go to Brookland Baptist most weekends to get a good word and give tithes and offerings. (I still don't understand the concept of tithes and offerings; stop lying to me telling me the money is for God, because God don't need money. Just tell me the money is for the operation of the church and I'm cool with that.)

I would also go to Muhammad Mosque Number 38 in Columbia because I love the discipline of the Nation of Islam and hoped a little bit of it would rub off on me. I was determined to be a righteous man. That meant no drinking, no smoking, and no casual sex. I wasn't even *cursing*. I also wanted my physical form to be right, so I was going to Gold's Gym three or four times a week to work out whatever devils were bothering me.

I will confess that I'd have a sip of alcohol from time to time because I was always doing promotions in the clubs and people would hand me drinks. Granted, I was an adult, and when you say no, people generally respect it, but sometimes it just seemed easier to accept the drink and keep things moving. I wasn't perfect, but I was damn near close.

I had been living clean for several months when I decided to text (texting was a thing by then) Mook Mook to tell her about my progress. She didn't text back. That's when I knew she really wasn't fucking with me. Even still, I resisted sleeping with any other women. I was convinced that if I set my table and became the man I felt like she deserved, then at some point God would direct her path back to me. If you want something, then you have to show and prove it through actions and deeds. You can't tell God you *want* your girl back but then be out there banging other women. You've got to demonstrate that you're serious. For a long time, I was.

That is, until I went to my best friend (to this day) DJ Frosty's crib. Frosty and I would work on all kind of projects together, like mixtapes, or parody songs I would play during my shift on Hot. Earlier that week at the station, my cohost Bill Black had introduced us to a couple of young ladies who were cool as hell. We laughed and joked with each other, and they ended up hanging out with us at Frosty's crib later that night. One thing led to another and someone came up with the bright idea to play "Strip Uno." The rules were basically if you lost a hand you either had to take a shot or strip. That left me in a bind because I really didn't want to do either. But the young ladies were there. The music was playing. I got caught up in the vibe. So I played a hand. And lost. I wasn't stripping, so I took a shot instead. My first in months.

As soon as the liquor hit my throat I felt immediate guilt. "Why did I do that?" I thought. I started experiencing a light panic attack. Everyone else was having a blast, but all I could think was, "The universe isn't going to let me get Mook Mook back. God isn't going to be pleased." The voices in my head would not shut the fuck up.

Meanwhile the losing hands started to pile up, so now I was sitting across from two young ladies in panties with their breasts out. The last few months of clean living were going down the drain fast. I lost again and took another shot. Having been sober for months, my tolerance was low. Soon I was really drunk.

The Jehovah's Witnesses call anyone who's not a witness a "worldly" person, meaning that they're not living the way God wants us to. I had become obsessed with this notion of "worldliness." I started telling everyone that we were living foul and God was not pleased. That we were all going to hell.

Everyone just laughed at me and kept playing. "Worldly" was exactly what they were trying to be that night. And then some. I couldn't take it anymore, so I stood up and made a break for home. I was heading out the front door before Frosty caught up with me. "What the fuck are you doing?" he demanded. "Don't leave. I can't handle all these girls myself. You're ruining everything."

"You can do it," I told him. "Have a blessed night. I'm out."

Frosty saw I was serious, so he tried another tack. "Look, you're drunk as hell," he rightly pointed out. "You can't drive home like this. Just crash on the couch and everyone will leave you alone."

He had a point. A DUI wasn't going to please God or Mook Mook. I figured he could handle the girls on his own and once I sobered up I would head home.

I went back in and made myself comfortable on the couch while everyone else kept partying in the next room. After a couple of minutes, a woman began calling my name in a low whisper. "Charlaaamagne . . . ," she purred.

"What?" I yelled back.

"Come here right now," she replied in the same low whisper. "We don't want to hear none of that Godbody shit! Get in here."

It was like the devil himself testing me.

Let the record show I failed his test.

Miserably.

Within seconds I was up off the couch and into a bed with two of the young ladies. Threesomes are most men's fantasies, but mine was turning into a nightmare. I felt like I was in the movie *The Devil's Advocate*, where people's faces took on slightly demonic qualities. That's how the two women looked to me. Not that the hallucinations stopped me. We immediately started having sex, though the act just further heightened my anxiety. "Which one am I supposed to focus on when I'm finishing?" I worried. "That one? Or both? What do I do?" I was having a panic attack in the middle of sex! I have a theory that only Satan causes confusion, so being confused over who to focus on was definitely the devil's work.

When I got home the next morning, I found myself in a full-blown panic attack. It was all those terribly familiar feelings.

Heart beating fast. Feeling frantic. Shortness of breath. Like I was Chicken Little and the sky was falling.

All because I had gotten drunk and slept with those women. I kept hearing Minister Farrakhan's voice in my head saying, "When a woman is lusting after you and offering you a night of wild sex, talk to her, tell her she's better than that, encourage her to be better. That's what a righteous man should do."

Granted, I'd tried at first, but I had ended up doing the exact opposite. Mook Mook would never get back with me now. It didn't matter if she knew or not. The universe knew. I once read a quote attributed to Albert Einstein that said, "Everything is energy, and that's all there is to it. Match the frequency of the reality you want and you cannot help but get that reality. It can be no other way. This is not philosophy. This is physics." (It turns out he didn't actually say it. But who cares? This is about the message, not the messenger.) I knew my energy hadn't matched up with the reality I wanted. I became convinced the sky was falling and the rapture was coming any minute. I thought Jesus was going to step out of the sky with the instrumental for Wu-Tang Clan's "Triumph" playing and teach me and the world a lesson.

If they'd had Twitter in 2004, I would have unleashed a tweet storm proclaiming that I was done with the world and I wanted to kill myself. I would have made Tyrese look in control and rational.

But in the absence of social media, I damn sure told all my homies that I wanted to kill myself. The exact words might have been, "I don't want to be here anymore." I don't know if I was exactly suicidal, but I was definitely feeling "fuck it all." I told Mook Mook the same thing, and she called my mom.

She in turn called my father, who drove ninety-four miles from Moncks Corner to Columbia to see what the hell was wrong. When he got there, I was sitting on the steps of my apartment with my head in my hands.

"What's the matter with you, boy?" he asked.

I couldn't articulate what I was feeling, so I just kept saying over and over, "I let God down, I let God down."

He asked me if I was high or drunk, but I shook my head. He'd been around enough substance abusers in his life to know I was telling the truth.

My father is not one to beat around the bush. After a few more minutes of me moaning that I'd let God down, my father started getting pissed. I knew I better get to the point, so I started downloading the situation. How I'd lost Mook Mook and had wanted to get her back by living right. How I'd spent months being sober and righteous but had then blown it all by getting drunk and having a threesome.

When I finished, my dad just stared at me for what seemed like an eternity. Finally he said to me, "So I drove a hour and a half because you had some drinks and got some pussy? If you're going to hell for getting some pussy and liquor, then I'm doomed too. Show me where the hell the girls and the liquor at because you done stressed me out with this bullshit."

I don't know why, but that calmed me down.

"The whole point of God Godding is that he forgives us for our bullshit," he continued. (You didn't read that wrong; my father definitely would say, "God be Godding.") That made sense to me. God forgives (even if Rick Ross doesn't). As it says in 1 John 1:9, "If we confess our sins, he is faithful and just to forgive us of our sins and to cleanse us from all unrighteousness."

199

I was happy to embrace the concept of forgiveness, but the Strip Uno situation was a strong reminder that if I wanted to avoid future panic attacks, I should simply do what God wants in the first place. I knew that in my heart, but it turns out I'd still have a few more missteps before I fully got on the right track.

#Cheater

I was eventually able to win Mook Mook back, but even after we were together again, I still didn't truly appreciate what I had. As we moved from city to city and I experienced more professional success, I began to slip back into my old habits. Despite all my talk about "letting God down," the truth is I had become a chronic cheater. I hated what my father's cheating had done to my childhood home, yet I was still bringing that same energy into *my* child's home. The apple was falling right at the base of the tree.

Looking back, more so than the devil, my cheating was really due to ego. Like so many men before me, I equated getting as much pussy as possible with being a "real man." As much as I didn't want to admit it, being fired so many times had been a blow to my ego. I viewed sleeping around as a way to reassert my masculinity and create a false sense of power. It was like my ego was screaming, "I'm not good enough for your station? You think I'm never going to make it? Well then just look at this bad chick I'm about to smash. Is that good enough for you?" It wasn't that I thought women were disposable. I always felt that sex was a special, intimate experience. I knew that there was a tremendous power that comes from a woman letting you inside her. I just didn't know what to do with that power.

Thankfully, I eventually learned that cheating on my wife was a terrible mistake, before she walked away from me for good. First of all, cheating created incredible levels of anxiety. You want to talk about a mind fuck? Nothing will have you more stressed out than cheating.

The lying was the worst. I'd tell a lie and then sit back and start stressing whether it was convincing enough. My wife might say cool when I made up some BS story about what I was doing at night while out of town, and I'd worry she really didn't believe it. "Maybe she's just seeing how deep a hole I can dig for myself before she busts me." I'd start beating myself up over telling a story with too many holes in it. "You idiot! Why didn't you cover your tracks better!"

Every time I created a fake meeting, or said I had to visit a friend, I felt like I was only inches away from getting caught. When you tell one lie, then you have to tell another lie just to back the first one up. Soon you're living in a house of cards constructed of deceit, which is one of the most fragile, shaky places you can find yourself. You know it's only a matter of time before the foundation gives out. How can you not experience anxiety knowing that eventually all this shit will be crashing down around you?

Outside of worrying about getting caught, I hated myself for what I was doing. You see, for all my bullshit, I have no problem being self-aware. I might not make the right choice, but I am honest with myself. I knew I was being a hypocrite. How could I claim to be a "real" person while constantly lying? I was a piece of shit. And knowing that sucked.

Especially because Mook Mook had been such a special partner. She had my back through each and every one of those firings. She was the one who'd always encourage me not to give up. She told me she'd love me no matter what happened. She was also the one who had a job and held the house down when I had no money coming in.

Knowing that I was taking a special woman for granted messed with my head. I was waking up anxious and going to sleep nervous. It was no way to live.

Finally, I asked myself, "Do I want a new piece of pussy or peace of mind?"

I chose peace of mind and have never looked back.

Peace of Mind or Piece of Pussy?

I know I don't deserve praise, or even credit, for doing something that I should have been doing since day one. I still want men reading this to understand just how powerful being faithful has changed my life for the better. I know you guys think you're happier when you're getting some on the side, but I promise you're not. Cheaters are like crackheads. They turn their lives upside down and inside out chasing a high that's never worth the collateral damage.

I see other guys out there and I know they're cheating. Just like my daddy could always tell when someone was hitting the pipe. Because we'd both been there. The guilt is like a stench on those guys. And if I can smell it, I know their old ladies are catching a strong whiff too. They have to be paranoid. They have to be miserable. They have to be tired of stacking lie on top of lie on top of lie.

My message to them is: kick the habit. Go cold turkey just like I did. I'm using all this drug terminology because when I stopped cheating, it literally felt like I was quitting drugs. I'm dead serious. All the stress and anxiety I was carrying around with me evaporated once I finally decided to keep my dick in my pants.

That's why I feel more powerful now than I ever have in my life. Being faithful is like working out, eating right, not drinking, and not getting high: you just feel better. It's an integral part of any healthy lifestyle. Trust me, brothers, the lying and the sneaking around is bad for your health. Emotionally and physically.

The good news is that being faithful isn't that hard. You just have to be clear in your goals and honest with yourself. For instance, traveling to LA used to be my worst nightmare. There were a couple of young ladies I would see out there, and every single trip would fill me up with anxiety. I was supposed to be focused on business, but 85 percent of my mental space was dedicated to planning on how I was going to cheat. I'm in town to meet with power agents and heads of networks, but all I can think about is how I'm going to convince my wife I'm back asleep at my hotel when I wasn't.

Today, I don't even play around. If I'm going to LA, my wife is coming with me. That way, instead of acting like I'm single for the night, I'm focused on what's in front of me: movie and TV scripts and building relationships. The opportunities that could change my family's lives forever. Plus, when I'm not working we have a fantastic time together. Mook Mook has friends out there now, so we all go out and eat together. As I mentioned, we sometimes get high, we get drunk, and we have fun. We make memories together, and that's what it's all about.

When I recently went to LA to interview Kanye, my wife was sick and ended up staying back in Jersey. Not a problem at all. I was all business. The day of the interview, I woke up at

2:00 a.m. and went to the iHeart studio in Burbank so I could be on *The Breakfast Club* in New York City. Once the show was over, around 5:00 a.m., I went back to the hotel, worked out, and then took a nap. Then I woke up, ate breakfast, and left for Kanye's crib around 11:00 a.m. I ended up staying with him till around ten that night. As soon as we were done, I went back to my hotel, grabbed a shower, and hit the sack. At 2:00 a.m., I was back up to tape another episode of *The Breakfast Club*. I'd gotten maybe four hours of sleep in two days, but I felt great! I had accomplished what I'd come out there to do, without getting sidetracked in the BS.

Imagine if I'd tried to sneak some side action into that day? I probably would have come up with some excuse on why I couldn't be at Kanye's till later in the afternoon. If I stalled on going over there, maybe I would have only gotten an hour to tape with him (we actually ended up taping for almost four). Or even worse, he would have lost interest (always a possibility with Kanye) and pulled the plug on the interview. I might have jeopardized what turned out to be one of the biggest moments in my career just so I could cheat.

I've seen guys do versions of what I just described. Push back meetings, no-show at events, or leave appointments early just so they can sneak some side pussy in. I'm telling you, they're just like crackheads. My question to those guys is, "For what?" Trust me, you gain more when you give your all to one good woman. I'm devoting myself to my wife and my kids and I've *never* been more blessed personally and professionally.

That's especially evident when a professional opportunity falls through. I'm able to deal with the disappointment much better than I did in the past. For instance, recently I found out that a network passed on a show I had been talking to them about. I ain't even tripping. I figured that for whatever reason the network wasn't the right home for me and eventually I'd find the right place. I was confident because I know I'm doing everything else correctly in my life. I'm treating people right. I'm giving out positive energy. That makes it much easier to handle whatever energy life throws back at me.

In the past it would have been a different story. My mind would have been clouded by all the anxiety and stress I was carrying around. I would have taken the rejection personally and doubted my talents. I would have said, "Fuck that network. They don't appreciate me. I'm never dealing with them again!" Plus, I would have felt like the negative energy I was creating by cheating was the reason things didn't go through.

Now that my mind is free of that anxiety, I don't take the rejection personally because I'm able to accept that it just wasn't meant to be at this particular network. A few weeks later I went back to the very same network with an idea for a scripted show and they bought it in the room. See, it literally pays to be faithful! Now someone might be reading this and saying, "Man, being faithful don't have shit to do with getting paid!" Well, I can only tell you what works for me.

The best part, of course, is simply being on the same page with my wife. She's the only person who knows what I truly need. What I want. And what's so beautiful is that no matter what happens, she stays balanced. If I'm riding an emotional roller coaster about potential deals or opportunities, she can't be fazed. If something falls through, all she'll say is, "You'll get 'em next time, babe." If something does come to fruition, all she'll say is, "That's great, babe." Her balance helps me stay level.

No matter what anyone says about me on social media, or

no matter what sort of slander gets thrown at me online, she never brings any of that back to me. None of it. Even if people call her up and say, "Did you see what Charlamagne got into this time?" She never sweats me about it. I mean, "Neva-eva-eva-eva" (word to Trillville).

All she does is support me. When my anxiety was really getting out of control, she was the one who pushed me to get help. "Baby, go to therapy," she told me. "You need to talk to somebody. Go. Go." All the progress I'm making I owe to her.

Fears of a Full-Time Father

Even though I've managed to ditch all the stress I was carrying from being unfaithful, I still carry a lot of anxiety connected to being a father. A little bit of parental paranoia just goes with the territory. Though I may need to work on my own level of it.

I seem to have a more severe case of parental anxiety than most. It started even before my first daughter was born. When Mook Mook found out she was pregnant, I felt anxiety over whether we should keep the baby. I loved Mook Mook and wanted to have a family with her, but the timing didn't seem right. I'd just started working for Wendy Williams's radio show in New York City, though I use the term "working" loosely. Yes, I had been on the show every day for a year and a half, but I had just started collecting a check. I was still living in a condo owned by Wendy's husband, Kevin Hunter. Mook Mook's situation wasn't any better, as she was living in her grandmother's apartment in a project out in Coney Island. I remember thinking, "Damn, is having a kid right now the smart thing to do?" It didn't seem like the best situation to bring a child into.

We went back and forth about the timing until one night we were lying in bed and I just blustered out, "We can't abort our baby. You know what I'm saying? We just can't. That just wouldn't fit right with me. Not us." Mook Mook agreed, and we decided to go ahead with it. Suffice it to say it was the best decision we ever made.

I still experienced a lot of anxiety during the pregnancy. I used to get very nervous about Mook Mook having to ride the subway all the way to Coney Island every day. The trip was over an hour and she was living in the projects. It seemed like a lot to ask a pregnant woman to deal with on a daily basis. I finally had a little bit of money coming in, so I found us a small two-bedroom apartment in Lyndhurst, New Jersey.

One night I was on my way to our new place and I got pulled over by the police at a roadblock by the Lincoln Tunnel. Turned out I had a suspended license and so they took me to jail. I was bugging because I thought, "Mook Mook is pregnant, we just moved into this new place, and we don't really know the surroundings and she might get lost trying to find me." I also didn't want her coming to the station because my paranoid mind kept flashing on news stories about police officers in New York assaulting women. Luckily, they ended up letting me out after a few hours and none of the nightmares I was imagining ever came close to happening.

There are a lot of unknowns about pregnancy that made me anxious. I was at the gym and I overheard two women on the treadmill talking about how one of their friends lost a baby at the seven month due to low amniotic fluid. I went home and made the mistake of googling it. Then I couldn't get it out of my mind. Later I read an article about Prince and saw his son died due to a rare condition called Pfeiffer syndrome. I became worried about that. Someone mentioned a friend who had suffered a miscarriage, and that became a fear. Every time I read about something terrible happening in someone's pregnancy, I worried it was going to happen to us.

We actually did have a serious situation with my second daughter. About a month before her due date, Mook Mook called me while I was on my way to tape my MTV show *Uncommon Sense*. Throughout the whole pregnancy she had been dealing with gestational diabetes and now her doctor had just discovered she also had placenta previa. If they didn't induce labor immediately, the doctor thought my baby and my wife could be in serious trouble.

"But since they know what they want to do, why don't you tape your show and then just come by the hospital when you're done," she told me.

I know this will sound strange, especially after all I've just said, but I didn't run straight to the hospital. Instead, I followed her instructions to tape the show first and then went. We knew what the problem was, and the doctors had a plan they believed in. I felt confident that everything would turn out fine—and it did. I realized then that when I'm faced with an actual emergency, I feel completely calm and in control and that it's only the unknown, the "what-ifs" that scare me.

Now back to my first daughter. Her birth went off without a hitch, and for the first hour or so of her life, I was calm. Just enjoying being in her presence and feeling proud of her mother. But when the nurses came in and took my newborn daughter to the nursery, all my anxieties came rushing back. "Why are you taking her away?" I asked one of the nurses. "Oh, we just need to run some tests on her to make sure everything's working all right."

I didn't like the idea of them taking such a small baby away from her parents. Didn't sit right with me. I rushed over to the nursery and posted up by the big glass window, trying to keep an eye on my daughter. Questions raced through my mind. Why weren't they asking me for permission to run the tests? Suppose they hurt her when they tried to take blood. Suppose one of the nurses was too rough while handling her. Worst of all, suppose one of the nurses was tired from being over-worked and accidently switched name tags with my daughter and someone else's baby! Suppose we took the wrong baby home and didn't realize it till years later. Or what if they put a microchip in my daughter when I couldn't see her? People have been saying the government has been putting in RFID micro-chips since 1983. That way they can track our every move and essentially control us. Sorry, not my baby! I wasn't going to let any of that happen on my watch!

I was so paranoid about all those scenarios that I just stared through that window until they finally brought her back a cou-ple of hours later.

I was scared out of my mind the day it was time to take our daughter home. Like so many fathers before me, I had no idea how to properly install a car seat. Suppose I strapped it in wrong and we got into an accident? The voices in my head were saying that maybe the seat might go flying out the window! Not taking any chances, I made Mook Mook sit in the back and hold the baby seat while I drove.

And man, I drove so carefully on that ride back home. Like I had three hundred pounds of cocaine stuffed inside a dead white woman in the trunk and a cop in my rearview mirror. My heart was racing and my hands were sweating as I gripped the wheel. I followed every traffic rule like I was a sixteen-year-old taking my driving exam.

I felt a huge sense of relief when we finally made it home, but it was just the beginning, as those first few days were filled with some of the worst stress I've ever felt. I deal with lack of sleep every week, but nothing prepares you for those early days. No one is sleeping, and everyone is on edge and scared. Every couple of minutes I had to stick my head in the baby's room just to make sure she was still breathing. Every time she cried, I thought she'd hurt herself. Every time she didn't cry for what seemed like too long, I worried about crib death. Every time she wouldn't nurse, I imagined she had some sort of disease that would stop her from eating.

Luckily, as she always does, my mother gave me some timely advice. "I don't know what the hell I'm doing," I confessed to her. "I have no idea how to take care of this child."

"Don't worry about it," my mother reassured me. "Just love her. That's all you have to do. Just love her."

Those simple words really helped. Because loving her was something I was already doing.

That reliance on love became the foundation of my approach to parenting. When my daughter grew older and started acting out a bit, I found myself mimicking how my parents had handled my outbursts. One time my daughter cursed and I immediately scooped her up and started spanking her. But even as I was doing it, I felt stupid. In that moment I understood the old saying "This is hurting me worse than it's hurting you."

After that, I decided I wasn't physically disciplining my kids anymore. Disciplining them, yes. Just not with force. I didn't want to subject her to what I'd gone through.

My parents used to beat the shit out of me when I was a kid. My mother's go-to move was slapping me in the mouth when I talked crazy. *Slap!* That was light work though. My father would really lay into me. I remember one time after I got my driver's license I was following him in a car while he drove his truck to handle some business. At one point I ran a stop sign, so he signaled me to pull over. I drove over to the side of the road and rolled my window down while he walked back to my car. When he got to me, without a word he leaned in and smacked me like Rick James slapped Charlie Murphy. "Wake up!" he yelled, and then walked back to his car. I was stunned, hurt, and shaken, but didn't dare say anything back to him.

The worst was when I was eleven or twelve years old and my mother caught me setting the rug in our trailer on fire with some matches. "Wait till your father gets home," she told me. Talk about fear. I spent the next several hours freaking out over what my father was about to deliver. He did not disappoint.

When he got home and heard what had happened, he went right to work. He proceeded to whip me with an extension cord. That heavy plastic sliced through my skin like a knife through butter. He wasn't done. Then he made me strip naked and take a bath. I don't know if you've ever had to get into hot water after getting whipped, but trust me, it's a special kind of pain. A kind of pain you remember for the rest of your life. Granted, setting rugs on fire inside a trailer is not something you want your kid to get in the habit of doing but there are other ways to teach that lesson other than beating him like you trying to make him say his slave name instead of "Kunta Kinte." Seriously, every time I watch a slave movie and see one of them getting beat with a whip, I think to myself, "Damn, he must have been trying to burn Massa's single-wide trailer down. . . ."

Outside of the lasting emotional scars I know it leaves, one of the reasons I've never wanted to lay my hands on my kids is because I'm obsessed with protecting them. Being the one who actually hurts them never made any sense to me.

Protect and Provide

I kept thinking I would get less anxious as my daughters got older, but baby swapping in the hospital was just the beginning of it. If I read about something terrible happening to a kid online, or see a story on TV, I'll immediately think the same thing will happen to one of my daughters. Once I saw a story about how the teachers at a day care were abusing the kids. Smacking them when they cried and touching on some of them. That terrified me. I couldn't stand the idea of something similar happening to my daughter, so I started popping up unannounced at her day care. I'd sneak up to the door and stand there like Tupac by the locker in *Juice*. Just staring. The teacher would sometimes look up and see me and I'd just stare back. "Yeah, that's right. I'm here surveying the scene," I told the teachers with my eyes. "You never know when I'm going to appear, so you better stay on point!" I'm sure they thought I was crazy, but in the words of Tupac's character in that film, "You're right, I am crazy, but you know what else? I DONT GIVE A FUCK!" Hey, when it comes to my kids, you damn right I'll be crazy.

It was the same when my daughter went to elementary

school. I'd pop up unexpectedly from time to time and just stare into the classroom. I never went in or tried to get my daughter's attention. I wasn't there for her. I was there to let those teachers know I was watching. That I was liable to show up at any time, without any warning. I'd still probably be popping up today, but it's gotten a little harder as she's gotten older. Now all the schools are on lockdown due to school shootings and you've got to call ahead before you can come. No more just rolling up to a classroom like I used to.

Ah yes, school shootings. That's another of my major fears. I'm always concerned that some disaffected white kid is going to show up to her school with a gun. I've gone to pick her up and asked myself, "What if some deranged white dude starts picking kids off as they are coming out the school?" I like to imagine myself running him over with my truck. That's how much thought I have given this. I know I shouldn't, but I worry about it all the time. From the moment I step onto school grounds, I'm on high alert for school shooters. Don't let a white kid with a faraway look in his eyes or, even worse, a trench coat on give me bad energy. There's no telling what I'd do. It's at the point now that I'm shook to death of potential white shooters period. Even outside of school grounds. A guy like Dylann Roof will do that to you. Almost anywhere I go these days, I've got my head on pivot for a pissed-off white guy about to pull a gun.

Another huge fear is someone trying to run up in my house and hurt my family. Every day I'm playing out scenarios in my mind where I thwart a home invasion. I'm too paranoid to tell you my plans, but suffice it to say, it never ends well for the bad guys.

That doesn't stop me from worrying about it though. Only a handful of people know where I live and I'm going to keep it that way. If you know my address, it's because I gave it to you. You're not just going to stumble upon our house. And you're certainly not going to get inside unless you've got a damn good reason to be there. When someone shot up one of the Waffle Houses in Tennessee and escaped after killing several people, I was a wreck. Every hour that terrorist was on the loose I was nervous. I even told my wife not to answer the door for any strangers. As if this guy with every cop in the South looking for him had somehow made it to New Jersey and was going to show up at my door. Didn't begin to make sense. Still, I had trouble sleeping until they caught him.

One of the biggest fights my wife and I ever had was when we were living in Teaneck. There had been a snowstorm and my wife called me to say that she'd just gotten home with our daughter to find our driveway was blocked. I told her that I would be home in twenty minutes and to just sit tight, I'd shovel it when I got back. After she hung up, a guy came walking down the street and saw that she couldn't get in the driveway. He offered to shovel it for her, and since she didn't want our daughter waiting in the car, she accepted. The guy shoveled out the driveway and when he was done, asked if he could have a glass of water. I suppose that's a legitimate request. Shoveling snow *is* hard work. (Though I would have told him to just suck on some snow if he was thirsty.) Of course, that's not what my wife said. Being a kind person, she invited the guy into our house and gave him a glass. He drank his water, said thank you, and went on his way.

When I got home I was shocked to see her car in our driveway. When I asked my wife what had happened, she told the story of the guy offering to help, including his coming in for a glass of water. When she told me that, I went absolutely ballistic.

"You let a stranger into our house! With our daughter here?" I yelled. "What were you thinking?"

"He just shoveled the driveway and was thirsty!" my wife shot back. "Stop being so paranoid!"

"I'd rather be paranoid than come home and find you guys tied up! Or even worse!"

Her father actually called while we were arguing. I was so hot that he could hear me speaking with a voice raised through the phone. Being a good father, he asked to talk to me and to see what was going on. When I got on the phone, I told him, "Your daughter just let another man, a stranger, in our house while our child was here and I wasn't home." There was nothing else to discuss. Her father completely agreed with me. Eventually I calmed down, but my wife got the message. I needed her to be more protective of our house, both for our safety and my peace of mind.

Now she's just as cautious as me. When we moved into our current house, my wife met the movers unloading our furniture while I took care of some stuff at our old place. While unpacking the truck, the movers started noticing some of the framed gold records I'd received from record labels over the years. "Hey, is your husband in the music business or something?" one of the guys asked my wife. There was something in his voice she didn't like. "Naw, he's not in the music business," she told him coolly. "He's just a fan. He collects stuff."

As soon as she was out of earshot, she called me. "Yo, baby, when you get here, just stay in the car for a minute. Don't come out until these movers leave."

"Why's that?" I asked.

"Nothin', it's just that these movers are looking at your stuff and asking me questions about what you do. I don't want them

215

to see you and then decide to come back here one day. Who knows what they'd try."

Man, I loved hearing that so much. Even if the fear is irrational as fuck, I would rather be safe than sorry. Or in this case, paranoid and protected. I don't know if anxiety is contagious, but she damn sure feels how I feel when it comes to those kind of situations and I'm here for it.

Outside of something happening to my family, my next biggest fear is something happening to me. Not because I'm so full of ego, but because I'd hate for my kids to grow up without a father. That's one of the worst things I can imagine.

Because I'm so afraid of not being there for them, I've turned into a full-fledged hypochondriac. In my mind, every stomachache is a potential tumor. Every time my leg feels stiff after going to the gym I think it might be MS. Every spot on my skin (yes, I still have some) might be skin cancer.

One of the times I felt most like a hypochondriac came after Pimp C died. I still remember the date—December 4, 2007. I loved UGK so I was devastated. What made it worse was Pimp had just come home from jail. The whole time I was doing "Free Pimp C" campaigns on air (which by the way I don't normally partake in "free such and such" campaigns because I truly don't know if those people deserve to be incarcerated or not) and then almost as soon as he was home, "Free Pimp C" turned to "RIP Pimp C."

The autopsy results would show that Pimp sadly died of a drug overdose, but when I first heard the news I somehow got it in my head that he had died of a heart attack. I was working with Wendy Williams at the time, and as soon as I heard the news my chest started hurting. We were on air and during the entire show I was trying to clear my mind and silently begging my body not to have a heart attack.

Somehow I made it through the show and hustled back to the condo that Wendy's husband, Kevin, had put me up in in New Jersey. I tried to lie down and rest, but my chest would not stop tightening up. Even worse, my heart was BEATING FAST AS FUCK. I couldn't understand it, but I was petrified. I tried taking a hot shower, but it didn't matter.

I was supposed to fly out to South Carolina in the morning to see my family, and all I could think of was that I was going to die of a heart attack that night and when I didn't show up at home the next day, they would come and find my body just like Pimp C. I couldn't stand the thought of that, so finally I said, "Fuck it," and went to the emergency room. When I got there a doctor asked me what was wrong and I immediately blurted out, "I think something is wrong with my heart, and Pimp C died of a heart attack today and I don't want to too." I'm sure they thought I was crazy, but I had just gotten health insurance from the radio station, so they had no choice but to take me seriously. Otherwise they probably would have had the police throw me out. They checked my vitals, and of course nothing was wrong. Then they gave me an EKG (electrocardiogram) for my heart, and once again I was all clear. After looking at my results, a doctor said, "By any chance have you had any caffeine or energy drinks today?"

"Oh, shit, I had a Red Bull when I started my shift," I replied.

"Well, I suspect that's what it is," he said. "In the future try not to drink Red Bull, it's full of caffeine and sugar and makes your heart beat fast."

"Oh, OK. No problem," I told him, and got dressed to leave.

It turned out Pimp C had died of an overdose of sizzurp—promethazine and codeine—yet there I was convinced that I was having a heart attack because of a mixture of caffeine, sugar, and anxiety.

Another really bad stretch was after my friend Combat Jack, the pioneering podcaster, died from colon cancer. I visited him before he passed and he told me that he'd been suffering strange symptoms—fatigue, cramps, and upset stomach—for months before he was diagnosed. By the time he found out what he was fighting, it was basically too late. His cancer had spread and he passed in just two months. He left behind four beautiful children.

After hearing Combat's story I *stayed* in the doctor's office.

Not long after that, I felt a little knot on my abdomen, so I went to the doctor. He told me that it was just a little hernia from lifting weights and that I shouldn't worry. When it didn't go away after a few weeks, I went back for another checkup.

"Just a hernia," he told me. "Nothing to worry about." Still, I couldn't get the idea that it was a tumor out of my mind. So I went to see another doctor, who told me the same thing: it's a sports hernia. I still didn't feel confident I was OK, and I went to see yet another doctor. After he told me it was hernia too, I finally calmed down.

Because I'm always worried I might suddenly die, I go extra hard trying to spend time with my family. My thinking is if I might not be here ten years from now, I need to spend as much time with the people I love now.

For example, I got back to New York from my trip to interview Kanye in Los Angeles at four on a Friday morning. After landing, I drove straight to Power to tape *The Breakfast Club* at

6:00 a.m. We wrapped up at 10:00 a.m., then I spent another hour interviewing guests for the next week's show. Then I taped *The Brilliant Idiots* podcast for another two hours. After sitting in Friday-afternoon traffic in Manhattan, it was close to 3:00 p.m. before I got home. I'd had maybe four or five hours of sleep in the last seventy-two hours. The smart thing would have been to kiss my wife and kids and then jump into bed.

That wasn't going to happen though. My daughter had a cheerleading competition the next morning in Philadelphia, which meant she needed to spend the night in a hotel in Philly. There was no way I was going to let my wife (who we'd just found out was pregnant with our third child) drive to Philly with my daughter by herself. So despite being jet-lagged and exhausted, I got in the car with them and drove down to Philly.

Yes, I could have passed on the trip and gotten some sleep, but it would not have been truly resting. I would have stayed up till ten that night making sure they arrived safely. Then I would have woken up at six the next morning to make sure they hadn't overslept and missed the competition. Even though I would have spent the entire weekend lounging around at home, I wouldn't have gotten any true rest because I would have been constantly worrying about my wife and kids. I wouldn't have felt comfortable and at ease until they were back home safe and sound. As exhausted as I was, it was better to just go with them.

I tend to experience parental anxiety at anything my daughter does where competition is involved. So far the worst have been track meets. When my daughter first started running, I felt she wasn't utilizing her full potential as an athlete. At her first race, when the gun went off she didn't fly off the starting line. She just kinda took her time and ended up finishing in the middle of the pack. No offense to those other girls, but she should have won that race.

That's a problem for me, because I believe if God gives you a gift, you have to make the most of it. It would be one thing if God had made her slow-footed, or uncoordinated. But that's not the case. She's fast.

So afterward I got on her ass. "I've seen you run harder and faster in our backyard!" I told her. "You can't waste our time and your time. Every time you compete, you have to do your best!" That's it, nothing more nothing less, just do your best.

When her next meet came around, we had a little pep talk, and I expressed to her again about the need to compete. She nodded her head, and when the gun went off this time, man, she smoked the entire field. It wasn't even close. The only time she lost all day was in the relay, when a girl from another team beat her by a few inches. She was a little upset after that, but I told her not to worry about it and that I was proud of everything she'd done that day. It was a great moment for both of us.

Making It Make Sense

With the help of my therapist, I've been able to find some strategies that actually have been working in my battle against parental anxiety. One of the best and easiest is to simply focus on the facts. While it's not unnatural that I worry about my children being kidnapped, I need to be realistic about the threat level.

According to the Department of Justice, the vast majority of kids who go missing are taken by other family members. The chances of being kidnapped by a complete stranger are about 1 in 300,000. That means there's a 0.0033 percent chance of it happening. Cleary not something I should be wasting too much brainpower on.

Same thing with school shootings. I'm always looking for the next potential school shooter, but I'm most likely just wasting my time. According to the *Washington Post*, the chances of having your children killed in a school shooting is roughly 1 in 614,000,000. The odds are so small that it'll happen that I'm not even going to bother calculating them.

I'm working to accept that I don't need to fight the stress that comes with parenting. Instead, I just need to use it constructively. "It is important to remember that having stress present in our lives is not the problem," Amber J. Seidel, a professor at Penn State, told CBS in a recent interview. "It's the inability to cope in healthy ways with the stress that is problematic."

That means if I feel the need to be vigilant, then I need to focus on the situations that are more likely to create actual damage. I need to teach my daughters to be careful around cars now. And when they're older, to never get in a car when someone has been drinking. I need to make sure they aren't left unattended around swimming pools before they know how to swim. Insist that they wear a helmet when they bike. And truth be told, probably the most helpful thing I can do is make sure *I* never text and drive.

When I'm reminded of these factual stats, it helps me refocus. It also gives me something concrete to work on. Instead of worrying about kidnappers, I can worry about driving safely at all times. That's constructive worry, not wasted worry.

Another constructive step I've learned I can take is creating family rituals. If I'm constantly worried about where my family is at all times, the best thing I can do is try to transfer that anxiety into activities with them. If I'm most relaxed when I'm with them, why not create even more reasons for us to be together?

That might seem like a fairly obvious approach, but growing up my family didn't do a whole lot of things together. Remember, we didn't celebrate holidays, so right there we were missing out on a lot. The only "family events" I can recall are when we would go to my grandmother Rosa Lee's house for dinner. Even then it was really just my mom and my siblings. I don't recall my father being there too often.

Now I want to create the same memories for my kids, but on a bigger scale. One way is taking my daughter to the movies now that she's older. Just her and Daddy. We've seen *Black Panther, Sing, Avengers: Infinity War, Incredibles 2*—we'll go to whatever is out at the moment. I never did that with my parents. She loves talking about the movie with me on the way home and she's the only person I don't have a problem explaining the Marvel universe to. I know for a fact she's going to remember those times as she gets older.

I'm also committed to going on as many vacations with my family as possible. That's something that wasn't an option for my parents, but I'm blessed to be in a position where I can make that happen. I'm the first person in my family to make any real money and my priority is helping the people I love to see as much of the world as possible. Recently we've been to the Caribbean, but I'd like to start taking family trips to Africa, Europe, and Asia. Let my kids see that this world is bigger than just the United States of America.

A family summer vacation is a must every year. When the last week of June rolls around, we are out. My oldest daughter and I both have birthdays that week, so why spend it in New Jersey when we can be on an island somewhere? The week of Thanksgiving we always go down to South Carolina. The grandparents love it and it's also important for my kids. I want them to have a relationship with nature similar to how I did growing up. I want them to see that the world doesn't have to always move at the same frantic pace as it does around New York City. See that people still say "yes, sir" and "no, ma'am." Basically get everything positive and nourishing from Moncks Corner that I did but, without all the BS.

Most important, I need to accept my children as they are. I don't want them to be influenced by me professionally. I'm afraid they'll want to get into the entertainment business, because I know it's a pipe dream for most people. Not to mention it's too cutthroat. Especially for women. I've seen how women get treated in entertainment. The casting couches. I'm not saying those things don't happen in other fields, but it's probably more prevalent in entertainment. There are so few slots available that people, especially women, feel like they have to do anything to make it. And sadly there are too many men in power ready to exploit that fear.

Right now my daughter wants to be a dentist. I think that's a great choice. She can have her own practice, which means being her own boss. She won't have to be asking men for raises. Maybe down the road she'll decide she wants to be a doctor. Or a lawyer. Any of those are great because they allow her to be her own boss and shape her own destiny.

If one day one of my kids came home and said they wanted to be an actress, or a singer, I'm not sure what I'd tell them. Would I tell them "Fuck your dreams"? As much as I might want to tell them that, I'd have to get over my fears for them and support them in that too. Just like I'd have to support them unconditionally if they told me they were gay, or wanted to convert to a religion I'm not familiar with, or wanted to get their eyebrow pierced. (By the way, the eyebrow piercing can't happen until they're eighteen and out of my house.) At the end of the day, it's their life and I can only support them.

And if for some reason there's an issue that we have trouble finding common ground on, then I'll drag all of us into therapy. I think having a mediator in family disputes can be very helpful. I won't rush it—I think there's a natural anxiety that comes with being an adolescent which isn't necessarily a bad thing. If you only do things in your comfort zone, you're not learning enough about the world. You need to be a little uncomfortable until you figure out who you are.

While I don't think I'll completely stop having parental paranoia, I do think therapy is helping me get a handle on the levels. I'm feeling extremely plugged into my family, which is more important to me than any other kind of success.

Parental Paranoia
Clinical Correlation
by Dr. Ish

If you never question, wonder, or worry to yourself if you're being a good parent, you're probably not being a good parent. The very nature of assuming responsibility for someone else's life induces a healthy fear, as it should. Especially if you feel you haven't been totally responsible in all areas of your own life, as most of us have not. It's a universal fear all good parents have; it's healthy. Feel it. Embrace it. Push through. I tell all my anxious parents, "As long as you're acting out of love, the decisions you make for your child will always turn out right."

This is a great chapter for so many reasons. Not the least of which is to see the rarity of a black man shouldering the awesome responsibility of being accountable to not only his wife and his children but also to himself. As ironic as it seems, Charlamagne's only able to do that now because of the challenges he had with his own father growing up. One of the key developmental milestones of becoming an adult is coming to realize that your parents are people too. They have the same fears and flaws that we all have. They make or have made some of the same misguided decisions we've all made, and they live with the same shame and guilt because of it. They're human. And the day you're able to sit down with your parents and have not a child-to-parent talk, but a man-to-man or woman-to-woman talk, will be one of the greatest days of your life because in that moment you'll not only gain a deeper understanding about who they are but ultimately, who you are. And the fact of the matter is that if your parents had been the parents you wanted them to be, you wouldn't be the person you need to be. In his moment of deepest despair, in the midst of contemplating suicide, Charlamagne's dad showed up. And even though he may not have been the dad he wanted, in that exact moment, he was the dad he needed him to be and delivered a sobering message, however crass, so simple and plain that he immediately understood and felt better. So if we're going to blame our parents for everything that they aren't, we also need to give them credit for everything that they are: lumps, bumps, bruises, and all.

A huge take-home here, especially for black men and women, is the issue of cheating. Everything we go through in life is to make us into the person we're supposed to be. Charlamagne shines such a great light on this when he mentions his challenges with cheating. Ultimately he came to know the truth about the question all women ask: "Why?" Cheating is the manifestation of an underlying symptom. The truth is that it has absolutely nothing to do with the person you're cheating on or cheating with and has everything to do with what it is you feel you're lacking in your life and what emotional void you're trying to fill in that moment. It's a selfish short-term fix for a long-term problem. The caution here is that people often will violate their values in order to meet their immediate needs. The anxiety you feel while you're doing it comes from the incongruence. Deep down you know that this is not who you are. You know you're acting outside your self, and once you're mature enough to realize that, you also realize that doing things to meet an immediate need while sacrificing your values in the process only leads to more problems than it solves and it only worsens your stress. Work on you and the cheating works itself out.

Another great takeaway from this chapter is the lesson to be learned from divorce. It's one of the single most disruptive forces in a child's life. Depending on the age of your child at the time it occurs it can leave kids with a lot of unanswered horrible questions and negative assumptions. Did they leave because of me? Was I not smart enough? Was I not good enough? If I didn't get into so much trouble they would have stayed. If they had loved me more they would have stayed. And ultimately, the worst possible assumption that a lot of kids going through a divorce come to: "If one of the people who was supposed to love me the most left me, then I must be unlovable." Divorce can cause your kids to have depression, anxiety, poor self-esteem, and anger issues, and depending on how it's handled, it can make them a setup for the exact same future relationship issues their own parents had. Kids learn what they live. They practice the behavior you model for them in the home. There's a lot of fallout. As a psychiatrist, the particular thing I see in adults with anxiety issues is that a lot of them are still struggling with deep resentment of their same-sex parent after a divorce, no matter how long ago it was. Charlamagne talks about it here. The idea of "not wanting to grow up to be like them" is both the most prevalent thought process and the most damaging to have simply because that's not how our brains work. Our brains don't think in negatives, only positives. When you say, "I don't want to be like them," your brain automatically removes the "don't" and proceeds to make you exactly like them. Why? Because what we focus on is what we feel. It's the exact same reason that the things we fear the most are the very things we tend to attract the most into our lives because those are the things we regularly focus on.

The key to conquering fear is to turn it into a wish. When I hear you say, "I don't want to be like them," I know what you really mean is "I wish I could be a good parent." Instead of lamenting what you don't want, focus on what you do, simply say what you want to be—"I'm going to be a good husband who doesn't cheat"; "I'm going to always be there for my kids"—then your brain has something positive to focus on with a great new question: "How can I be better?" It will ultimately give you a greater answer and richer, more fulfilling life experiences.

CHAPTER 7

Fear of Failure

"It was a verse about fear of failure, which is something that everyone goes through, but no one, particularly where I'm from, wants to really talk about. . . . But facing up to that kind of feeling can be a powerful motivation to change. It was for me."

—Jay Z discussing "This Can't Be Life"

I'm a major comic book fanatic. And by comics, I mean Marvel. Sorry, I will never forgive the DC film universe for introducing the *Justice League* in an email attachment in *Batman v Superman*. What lazy-ass writing.

I grew up poring over Marvel classics like *X-Men*, *Black Panther*, *X-Force*, *Luke Cage*, *X-Factor*, and *Iron Man*. I'm so committed to Marvel that I have Wolverine tatted on my right arm. (My tattoo is trash and I should get it redone, but at my age I won't pay for anything that causes me pain.) In 2017, I even got to write and star in my own Marvel special comic called *Charlamagne Tha God's Marvel New Year's Eve*. It featured various Marvel villains linking up to crash a party I was throwing for having given Harry Osborn from *Spider-Man* "Donkey of the

Day." It was incredible and an experience I'm proud to be able to cross off my bucket list.

As a kid, I would often wonder about what sort of secret power I would have if I were a superhero. Would I be able to read minds like Professor X? Possess superhuman strength like the Hulk? Shoot lasers out of my eyes like Cyclops?

None of those skills ever did manifest themselves, but as I enter my fourth decade, it's clear I've had a secret power all along:

My anxiety.

I've possessed paranoia so potent it was able to help me leap right over the pitfalls that were waiting for me in South Carolina. That tripped up so many other African-American high school dropouts who were dealing drugs. The trifecta of failure my father infamously labeled, "dead, in jail, or being broke under a tree."

I was petrified by all three of those options. My peers were increasingly getting hooked on drugs, winding up in jail, or getting buried six feet deep. I was headed down the same path, but my fear of failure motivated me to cut the cord from the street lifestyle before I wound up like them.

Like any good superhero, I kept my superpowers hidden. I went out of my way *not* to seem scared. I wore a cloak of faux fearlessness that seemed to proclaim, "This guy really don't give a fuck!"

For a long time, that's how the world saw me. Cocky. Aggressive. Fearless. Hell, that cape looked so good on me it's how I saw myself too most of the time. And for many years, that cloak seemed to keep me protected.

My faux fearlessness served me well in an industry that can be as ruthless and unforgiving as the streets. All those times I was fired from radio stations despite strong ratings and support from the community. Each time, however, my fear of failure was so strong that I refused to quit or even let my discouragement show.

To the world, the only energy I projected was "on to the next one." I refused to reveal any vulnerability or sense that I was worried about what my future might hold.

Inside, of course, it was a different story. I was absolutely terrified of failing. Terrified not only that I might not reach the heights I aspired to but also that I was unemployed and back living with my mother in Moncks Corner. I was literally only steps away from being under those trees my father had warned me about.

I didn't even like picturing that possibility. The image would send shivers down my spine. So I'd push that thought to the back of my mind and get back to projecting confidence. The confidence that each time would ultimately lead me to an even better position than the one I'd been let go from.

If I hadn't been so afraid to fail, I would have never made it to where I am today. It's that simple.

Yet, while that fear of failure served me very well—it was only up to a point. Not unlike Captain America's strength, my superpower ultimately proved to have its limitations.

My life has changed a lot in the last twenty-some years. I'm not running from the cops anymore. I've gone from the trap to the cul-de-sac. Professionally, I've gone from getting fired from overnight shifts to being syndicated worldwide. My circumstances have changed dramatically. But my motivation has remained the same.

There's a quote from Will Smith's character in the movie *After Earth* that really summed up my situation. "Fear is not real. . . . It is a product of our imagination. . . . Do not misunderstand me. Danger is very real, but fear is a choice."

For a long time, my danger had been real. But even after the threat was gone, I was still making the choice to live in fear.

Now that I'm settled into my life and comfortable with who I am, I'm striving to make a different choice. Being anxious all the time doesn't serve the same purpose anymore. Through therapy, I've learned to let go of the fears that don't take me anywhere positive.

For instance, I'm anxious as I'm writing this right now. Why? Because I'm on a plane flying back from a family vacation in Anguilla and all I can think about is this thing crashing.

And when I'm not thinking about crashing, I'm thinking about what might happen if we encounter a racist TSA agent while going through customs. And when I'm not thinking about TSA agents, I'm worrying about all the text messages I'm missing while my phone is on airplane mode.

What I can do now that I couldn't do before is identify those fears as irrational. For instance, the odds of dying in a plane crash are one in eleven million (granted, dealing with a racist TSA agent is probably much higher). There's no point spending an entire flight worrying about it. I accept that the thought might cross my mind, but I can't let it sit down and get comfortable. Most important, I can't let it stop me from getting on the plane in the first place. It can't prevent me from taking my family on a beautiful vacation and expanding my children's view of the world.

There's no use working myself up over unlikely scenarios, because they're out of my hands anyway. All I can do is be ready to deal with whatever life throws my way. If there's a problem with the plane, all I can do is hope Captain Sully has come out of retirement and is in the cockpit. If I get hassled by a racist TSA agent, I'll be able to deal with it. I've encountered worse. And if something crazy happened and my phone is blowing up, I'll deal with it when I get home.

Therapy hasn't erased anxiety from my life—to paraphrase what they used to say about Michael Jordan in the nineties, you can't stop anxiety. You can only hope to contain it.

But therapy has done a much better job on my anxiety than Bryon Russell (do your googles) was ever able to do guarding Jordan. It's helped me understand that even if my natural tendency is to fret over the worst-case scenario in every situation, I don't have to *stay* in that space. When I was selling dope, that wasn't so irrational. The worst-case scenario was often the most likely one too. But that's not the case anymore.

Letting go of unhelpful habits is becoming a major theme in my life. I recently celebrated my fortieth birthday and my great friend Pastor Carl Lentz sent me a message encouraging me to pray about leaving "old things" behind. He explained that meant letting go of my old perspective on the world. It was time for me to expect good people, not bad, to come into my world. Time to expect good things, not bad, to fill up this new chapter of my life. God, he explained, never ever calls us into a new season without also supplying the grace to SUSTAIN US IN THAT SEASON.

Pastor Carl also told me—and I don't think he'll mind me sharing this—that there is an individual he would like me to connect with for mentorship purposes. Not me mentoring them, but them mentoring me.

I can't mention his name, but it's an older brother who is much more successful than I am. Pastor Carl told the guy that while I had already accomplished a lot, I could still use someone with reason and wisdom to learn from. Since the guy is in that place of life where all he wants to do is help, Pastor Carl thought we should connect.

I love Pastor Carl for that because he understands that WE NEVER STOP NEEDING HELP. We all need mentors, therapists, pastors, elders, partners—anyone we can lean on every step of the way! No matter where we are in our journey, we all need someone to lean on.

That's a message that's also been echoed in my therapy sessions. I came into the process thinking that I was the only one experiencing these kinds of thoughts. My therapist quickly helped me understand that I'm part of the rule, not the exception. That was a huge breakthrough, because when you suffer from anxiety, you tend to suffer alone. Because you don't have anything to put what you're experiencing in context, it's hard to accurately identify what you're going through. So you chalk it up to other issues. You think you're a pussy. Or a coward. Or bitch-made. You figure if you can just get a little tougher, a little more masculine, then the fears will go away. But of course they won't.

You may think you're a coward, but I'm here to tell you that you're not! You're only a coward if you run from your anxiety. As long as you're talking about it, you're a true tough guy.

Still Failing

One type of anxiety I still have to work extra hard to contain is the fear of failure. Even though I'm living my dream, there are still many moments when I feel the fear of failure sneaking up on me again.

Probably the most instructive example is a situation that

arose from my friend Lil Duval's infamous appearance on *The Breakfast Club*. The trouble started after I asked him how he felt about our celebrity-in-chief Donald J. Trump's proposal to ban transgender troops from serving in the military. Duval said something to the effect of "I don't care, I'm just doing my thing, shout out to all the trannies out there." Might have seemed like a harmless comment, but the term "tranny" is considered a slur by transgender people (which I suspect a lot of us only recently found out). I had only asked him because comedians usually have interesting takes on social issues, but a slur is a slur. I should have shut things down right there.

The interview kept going, however, and I wasn't quite ready for what transpired next. My cohost DJ Envy asked Duval what he would do if he started having sex with a woman and found out later in the relationship that she was transgender. "This might sound messed-up," replied Duval, "but I don't care, she dying."

Duval is a comedian, but that energy didn't feel right. I don't wish death on anyone except pedophiles, racists, and rapists. So I pushed back a bit, saying, "That's a hate crime, you can't do that."

Duval replied, "I can't deal with that. No, you manipulated me to believe in this thing. In my mind, I'm gay now . . . I can't live with that, bro, this would never happen if this never happened. So you don't have to worry about me killing nobody."

At that point I jumped back in and said I believed that a transgender woman who didn't disclose to her partner that she was born male should go to jail. (While I don't support anyone lying to a sexual partner, since I've learned more about issues in the transgender community, I don't think jail is an appropriate response for those sort of situations anymore.)

Duval agreed and said, "There should be some kind of repercussions for that if you do that to somebody, until then I'm going to have my own repercussions."

So I interjected again and said you can't go around killing transgenders. Duval replied—if someone did that to me and they didn't tell me, I'm going to be so mad I'm probably going to want to kill them.

Ouch.

At that point the conversation was a complete and total fail. I should have edited it out of the interview, but I didn't do it. Why not? That's a question I asked myself a lot after the interview went viral and we were rightfully attacked for promoting hate speech and violence.

The answer is that while I felt Duval's joke (and I do believe it was a joke) didn't have the right energy, I wasn't empathetic enough to the transgender community to realize just how hurtful it was. I should have realized how much hearing a comment like that, even made in jest, would upset people. But I failed to do it. Plus my nervous laughter just made things worse.

Contrary to popular belief, I'm not in the business of hurting people. I don't derive any pleasure from it. And it's certainly not good for our show.

The truth is I let the fact that Duval is my friend cloud my judgment. I know Duval would never hurt a transperson. I knew that he had even hosted a podcast with his gay sister that spoke on a lot of LGBTQ issues. Everyone else, however, didn't know that. All they heard was violence and hate.

Like I said, we were rightfully slammed in the press and online for what was said. We were threatened with boycotts. Two transgender activists interrupted my appearance at a political convention. The transgender activist and author Janet

Mock, who had just appeared on *The Breakfast Club*, slammed the show's "deplorable rhetoric."

There was a lot of backlash, and all of it was warranted. I'd known better than to continue that conversation, but I'd done it anyway. I'd failed myself and I'd failed many other people too.

First and foremost, I'd failed the transgender community. I'd laughed at their plight the same week a transgender woman named Troy "Tee Tee" Dangerfield was murdered in Atlanta. I'd also failed my show, which I truly try to use as a platform of positivity. And I felt like I'd failed Duval, since I could have redirected the conversation and saved us from going down a dead-end path.

The weeks after that interview were difficult, but I was determined not to wallow in my failure. Instead, I tried to learn from it. First of all, I gained a much-needed sense of compassion and empathy for the transgender community. The truth is I didn't know how much violence they encounter. More than twenty-five transgender women were killed in 2017. The majority of them were women of color.

My failure also reminded me of the importance of listening to my inner voice. I might not have been aware of the extent of violence against transgender women, but I knew joking about killing people is wrong. My inner guide understood that and I didn't listen.

If I'd been in a clearer state of mind that day, the rest of the interview could've turned out completely different. Learning how to stay connected to that inner guide is one of the skills I'm developing through therapy. Too often I've let the anxiety drown out my gut instinct. That definitely happened during the Duval interview. My therapist has taught me that when I'm feeling anxious, one of the best things I can do is focus on taking deep breaths. There are many different techniques, but the most basic one is to simply sit down in a chair with your back straight. Then take a deep breath through your nose while you count to five. Hold it for another two counts. Then breathe it back out your mouth while counting to five. Do that ten times in a row and I promise you'll feel much more at ease.

And really commit to that process too. Don't just breathe in and out for a few seconds and then wonder why you don't feel better. Slow down and really count out your inhales and exhales. Feel your stomach expand on the inhale and then feel your breath slowly leave your body on the exhale. It's a process, and you have to take it seriously to get results.

Obviously I can't stop an interview and take ten deep breaths when I feel off, but I can commit to doing breathing exercises throughout the rest of the day. I can commit to making breathing exercises part of my lifestyle. That way I won't need to calm down in a tense situation but will already *be* calmed down.

I try to fit them in several times a day. Maybe some in the morning after my prayers, while I'm driving to work, or before I go to bed. It's incredible how much peace we can create for ourselves just by focusing on our breath. To be clear, deep breaths can't replace therapy or medication if you need it, but adding them into your routines can make a big difference in those little moments of panic.

Don't Freak Out, Just Focus

A great example of how you can let a fear of failure get in the way of your success is the YouTube interview I did with Kanye before the release of his album *Ye.*

We both seem pretty calm in that interview, but trust me, there was a lot of nervous energy surrounding that situation. I didn't have anxiety about conducting the interview itself, that was easy for me. It was just a conversation, something I've always been comfortable doing.

The issue was that we're both nervous people and our anxiety rubbed off on each other. We managed to record the interview itself without any issues, but we started getting nervous about what to do with it. Two people with anxiety shouldn't be allowed to make decisions when they are both anxious about something, yet that's what we were faced with. There were all sorts of questions about how it should be edited and color-corrected. Then we had to decide when we wanted to release it. We had a lot of decisions to make and we overthought them all.

Personally I know when you're anxious about something, the last thing you want to do is move off emotion. That's when you'll make a mistake. Instead, you want to be as strategic as possible.

In this case, when I realized I was being overly anxious about the video, I thought of another exercise my therapist recently taught me. She said whenever you feel like all you can hear is anxiety in your head, put a mint in your mouth. But instead of chewing it right away, just let it sit there. Close your eyes and just focus on the mint sitting in your mouth. Think about what it feels like, what it tastes like, what sensations it creates. Focus on that mint instead of the anxiety that's making a racket in your brain.

I did that exercise whenever I found myself freaking out over the interview release, and it was strangely effective. It gave my mind a moment to be still. To press pause. And when I was able to get out of my emotions, I was able to remember what I've always known: it's going to be all right.

Over time I've learned that interviews are like pieces of art. They're created and then given away to the public. Once that happens, they don't belong to the artist(s) anymore. They belong to the people, who can either celebrate them, tear them to shreds, or ignore them. It's completely up to the public. As an artist, what you have to try to do is stay level-headed and remember that you're never as good as they say you are, just as you're never as bad as they say you are either.

Once I was able to calm all the way down, I stopped worrying about the "right" way to release the video and just accepted that no matter when or how it dropped, people were going to react however they reacted.

I don't think Kanye ever figured out how to calm himself down in relation to that interview. And while he never told me this, I suspect the reason he went on TMZ the same day we released it was because he was anxious about how people were going to react to the Donald Trump comments he made. He wanted to get out in front of them, but he was moving off of emotion. Instead of strategy. As a result, he ended up digging himself an even deeper hole after he made his infamous "slavery was a choice" comments. If he would have been able to press pause on his anxiety and put the interview out without any additional fanfare, he probably would have avoided a lot of drama.

In the end, however, I think the interview dropped right on time anyway. Lost in all the hype was the fact that it was released on the first day of May, which is Mental Health Awareness Month. The Trump and slavery comments got the headlines, but I thought Kanye did have a lot of important things to say about anxiety and mental health. It takes a lot of courage in hip-hop for a man to admit that he was so anxious about his weight gain that he got liposuction.

It also took a lot of courage for Kanye to admit that the competitiveness of the hip-hop industry caused him to suffer a nervous breakdown. "Fear. Stress. Control. Being controlled. Manipulation," he replied when I asked him what exactly had him feeling insecure. "Stressing things that create validation that I didn't need to worry about as much . . . just the concept of competition and being in competition with so many elements at one time. On a race against time, your age . . . yo, you getting old."

Trust me, Kanye is far from alone in having those feelings. So many rappers I know are consumed by those same fears. That they're getting old in a young man's game. That they're growing beer bellies and sporting gray hairs while the other rappers in the game seem to get younger and younger. A lot of them are terrified that they're going to be overtaken. Made irrelevant. That they're going to fail.

They just don't have the courage to say it.

Kanye did.

I believe that admission was a very powerful gift for hip-hop. It will give a lot of other rappers the freedom to open up about their fears and insecurities. That's good for the culture because it makes for better art. No one wants to hear about forty- and even fifty-year-old rappers bragging about what car they have or selling coke. We want to hear how they've evolved. Not stayed the same.

It's also good for the listeners because it allows them to be more open about their own insecurities. They might not be in the rap race, but there's some part of their life they feel anxious about. There's some part of their life in which they don't feel young enough, sexy enough, popular enough, or talented enough. When they hear Ye talking about those sort of fears, it lets them know that they're far from unique in having the same feelings. And that they can begin to deal with feelings of inadequacy and insecurity, instead of trying to act like it's "all good" all the time.

I understand a lot of folks want to "cancel" Kanye for his Trump comments or the slavery comments. I strongly disagree with him about Trump. And as someone whose directly descended from the slaves he was talking about, I know their condition was never a choice. I can still feel their rebellion in the South Carolina air.

But to "cancel" Kanye is counterproductive in my opinion. We've got a lot we can learn with him as he continues to learn more about himself. My hope for Kanye is that he simply follows the instructions he shared with me later in the interview.

"You've gotta stay brave. You have to follow your gut feeling," he told me. "I've gotta follow my gut. When I have that fear, I say, I have to be, you know, brave."

That's it. We all are going to feel fear. We just have to be brave and face it head-on. When we do that, it's called having faith. With that we can get past anything.

Speak Your Success

A lot of people who have a fear of failure make things worse by constantly downplaying themselves. They're so worried about failing that they try to lower expectations through self-deprecating comments. If they have a big test coming up, they'll tell their friends, "This teacher is so hard. I know I'm going to fail." If they're about to start a new job, they'll say, "This is a really cutthroat firm. I can't believe they even hired me in the first place. I'm sure I won't be here long." If they meet a guy they like, they might say, "He was cute, but I don't think I'm his type."

They can be well prepared, extremely talented, and beautiful, but they will talk themselves out of success because they're trying to soften the blow of failure. They'd rather announce they failed at something before they start than actually try.

I try to do the exact opposite. All I scream is success!

When I was doing night shifts in Charleston, I wouldn't stop talking about how I was going to be a radio legend. "I'm going to be a superjock!" I told my coworkers. "I'm going to be on the same level as Doug Banks (RIP), Tom Joyner, Angie Martinez, and Wendy Williams!" My coworkers probably found me annoying at best, arrogant at worst. But I had to talk like that. I knew how deep my fear of failure ran. If I wallowed in it, I would drown. I had to get past it by talking about success as much as possible. Even if it turned some other people off.

I did the same thing when I landed at *The Breakfast Club* on Power 105.1. Within days of starting there, I told anyone who would listen that we were going to become the top nationally syndicated show in the country. For a while I was pressing the station to use the part of Nicki Minaj's "Moment 4 Life" where she says, "Best believe that when we're done / This moment will be syndicated," as our theme song. People told me to chill and take things gradually, but I was insistent on talking about my belief in the show as much as possible. Today, we are the number one hip-hop show in the country, syndicated on more than 80 plus stations and 150 countries via Armed Forces Radio. Obviously that didn't only happen because I said it would; a lot of preparation, effort, and teamwork is what got us to that position. But for someone who fears failure as much as I do, expressing that confidence out loud played a big role in it too.

The person who really showed me how to take it to the next level is Tiffany Haddish. She never stops talking about what she wants out of life. It's to the point that when photographers are taking pictures of her, instead of saying "Cheese," she says, "Success!" She'll even end her live shows by "cursing" the audience with success.

I love that approach. You have to breathe success, walk success, and talk success constantly if you actually want to live it. Your whole aura needs to announce, "SUCCESS, SUCCESS, SUCCESS!"

This is why I constantly tell the universe, "I am a great husband! I am a great father! I am the biggest media personality on the planet! I am healthy! I am doing everything in my power to be the best me that I can be!"

I might not always feel like the best husband, father, media personality, or healthiest person. But I sure as hell tell the world I am. Because I know low expectations only lead to poor results.

Lasting Happiness

When I was last down in Anguilla at a villa I'd rented, surrounded by my friends and family, I was sitting by the pool getting my hair cut when I started to feel an unfamiliar sensation wash over me. For a few minutes, I felt off, but in a good way. I wasn't high, but I didn't feel sober either. Was I hallucinating again? Then I realized what I was experiencing was simply an extended feeling of peace. Of serenity. Of happiness.

It was still there later that afternoon when I went snorkeling with my man Van Lathan. I was awed by the brilliant colors and graceful movements of the fish darting in and out of the coral. Afterward we stood in the surf and wondered why fish don't seem stressed by our presence in the water (because we're on their turf). Then I took a walk along the beach with my daughters at dusk. We watched the sunset while pelicans dive-bombed for fish (or maybe fish aren't worried about us because we're not pelicans) just outside the break. I wasn't thinking about work that had to be done, worrying about what I was missing on Twitter, or whether a deal was going to go through. I was just happy. And it felt great.

A lot of you might be saying, "Shit, I'd be happy too living the life in Anguilla." And I hope you'll get the chance to. But my point was I've done all those things in the past, but the happiness I experienced was always fleeting. The sun would shine through for a moment or two, but then the clouds of my anxiety would block it out again.

Whether it's on vacation, or just hanging around the house with my family, I'm noticing that the moments of happiness I experience with my family are starting to last longer. To feel more real. And to occur with more and more frequency.

I've also learned that those clouds of anxiety are never going to go away forever. Literally the day I returned from my vacation, several old clips of mine began bubbling on Twitter. They were meant to address difficult issues in a transparent way, but they ended up hitting the wrong notes. So I apologize to anyone impacted or triggered by my words. For many years, I was edgy and risky with my words on my mic. I pushed the envelope on topics like sex. People would listen to me and say, "Man,

Charlamagne is *wild!*" There's a reason *Rolling Stone* called me the hip-hop Howard Stern.

Today, I have a much different mind state. While I'm always going to be authentic with my life's experiences, I'm embarrassed by things that I've said in the past. There are moments when I want it all wiped from the internet. I cringe thinking about my daughter watching some of my old clips. But I can't surrender to those fears.

I've come to accept that I can't be a prisoner of my past. Because the truth is, largely with the help of therapy, I've evolved a great deal over the past few years. I'm not the same thoughtless instigator I used to be.

This book, at its core, is about the power of evolution. About how we all have the ability to unpack all the bullshit, drama, negative energy, and pain we've been carrying around—and causing—for years and years and finally move on with our lives. To allow ourselves to be free and grow into the beautiful person that's always been inside us. I truly believe all of us are capable of that sort of transformation.

I do worry, however, that collectively we don't always give people the space to make those transformations. If Malcolm Little were alive today, would we have allowed him to become Malcolm X? Or would we have kept focusing on his drug dealing, gambling, and prostitution rackets? Would we have kept Malcolm Little down and not given him the chance to blossom into Malcolm X?

That's perhaps the greatest example of what personal evolution can look like, but there are so many others out there, in all different walks of life. If you are one of those people, I want to encourage you to keep pushing and bettering yourself, even if it feels like you can never truly detach yourself from things you might have done or said that didn't reflect your best self.

Personally, I can attest that it's incredibly stressful to have to come to terms with moments from your past that you're not proud of. I'm doing it right now and my anxiety, despite all the skills that I've picked up in therapy, is through the roof. I'm constantly trying to move beyond the old me, and every time I feel like I have, that old me says, "Nope bring your ass back down here with us for a little bit longer." It can be very frustrating, but ultimately it's part of the process. Every day I go to work on being a better me. Every day I look in the mirror and say, "*I am a damaged individual who is working on healing my pain.*" If you feel a little bit of truth in that declaration, then try saying it every day too. That simple statement will give you the courage and the motivation to break whatever stagnancy you're stuck in and start moving forward.

So Many of Us Hurting

And, as the saying goes, "Hurt people hurt people." Don't let those hurt people pick at wounds you have worked hard to close. If you have learned from your mistakes and have grown from your experiences, don't look back. You might turn into the proverbial pillar of salt—word to Lot's wife!

If someone is trying to pull you down or hold your back, stand firm in your knowledge of self. Know where you've been, where you are, and where you're going. And if you need to take your good friend anxiety with you on your journey, then do it! Let that fear of all the old shit people can use against you be your fuel to never be those things you don't like about yourself ever again. Your behavior might have been shitty, your language might have been shitty, your attitude might have been shitty, and the way you treated people might have been shitty, but if you have learned from it and are a better person now, then you are moving in the right direction.

The reason you don't want to hear those old stories about yourself is because you are scared. That's fine. Remember that life's greatest lessons are usually learned at the worst times and from the worst mistakes. Every once in a while God may tap you on the shoulder to remind you of those mistakes simply because he doesn't want you to repeat them. Let that fear of repeating your past mistakes keep you from making new mistakes, because if you are not learning from the sins of your past, you will always be a prisoner of your past. And you will serve a life sentence of being a "shook one."

Fear of Success and Failure Clinical Correlation by Dr. Ish

One of the takeaways from this chapter is Charlamagne's ability to heed the call to normalcy! A very valuable tool we use as therapists for clients who are engaging in atypical or flat-out self-destructive behavior is socialization. We want them to be exposed to as many "normal" or functionally socialized people of their same age as possible in the hopes that they will pick up on the social cues being used and learn what's acceptable social behavior and what's not. The goal is that the group will push back whenever they do something awkward or socially unacceptable and the client will then naturally autocorrect their behavior. When you have the ability to check your own behavior it's a more powerful tool because the reason for change is coming from an internal reference point, which is you. As a result the change tends to last longer and becomes much more effective in improving your quality of life.

A critical element of his personality that allowed him to rise above the fray is that he is self-aware. Self-awareness allowed him to look at himself through an objective lens and make a key observation. The key insight was that the life course he saw taking shape for himself was incongruent with the person he knew himself to be. True, you have to know you're worth more, but it's even more cellular than that. Your inner thoughts have to match the emotions you feel, which have to match the behavior you manifest. It must all be in line. It must all be congruent. If one part of that triad doesn't match, you feel this thing we clinically call dysphoria. It's a hard-to-describe feeling that's a combination of many things, including anxiety, depression, irritability, and agitation, and all you know is that something just doesn't feel right. To bring himself back in balance Charlamagne made the hard choice, which was to be his true self. A lot of people don't yet know who they really are and don't honestly believe they have value or something to offer the world, so that choice to change and become more isn't a choice they can actually see. A choice unseen is a choice never taken. In that moment you rob yourself of becoming all you can be and you rob the world of experiencing the gift you came here to bring. Nobody wins.

The "fear of success" is a well-worn phrase among therapists and in pop culture alike to help people become aware that they may actually be playing an important role in why they may not be succeeding on their chosen life path. When I hear someone say they have fear of success I know what they really have is a belief problem. They don't honestly believe they're worth being successful or worth having the life they say they want. They don't believe they're capable of doing it. They don't believe they'd be accepted and embraced and fully loved if they became that. In therapy we call this a classic self-limiting belief system and this can manifest in your life in a number of ways. One way is as negative self-talk. You tell yourself self-defeating things in an effort to lower expectations and lessen the blow of any disappointment if you don't reach that goal you set for yourself, or worse yet you talk yourself out of even trying in the first place. Or it can also show up in your life as classic self-sabotage behavior. These are the head-scratching stories you hear about when people do something that makes you say to yourself, "I wonder why they did that?" or "What were they thinking?" The term "self-sabotage" means you show a repeating pathological pattern of behavior that doesn't allow you to take the next step forward and shows up right at the very moment when it seems that next step is readily available to you. It also comes from the lack of belief you have in yourself and your worth. In order for you to have the life you say you want, you not only have to find a way to take action and break through that patter that first time, but you also must consistently reinforce to yourself the belief that you, in fact, are worth it, that you deserve it, and that you belong, by showing up and continuing to take action over and over again until your new positive pattern starts to run on automatic like your old negative pattern used to.

A big shift in therapy comes when you're able to delete the negative self-talk and replace it with more positive self-talk. I absolutely love the positive self-talk or affirmations Charlamagne uses with himself on a daily basis. Sometimes our minds seemingly play tricks on all of us but the truth of the matter is that your brain is your friend and will believe what you actively tell it to believe. With constant repetition it's simply a matter of time before what you think or the things you believe start to change the way you feel. The way you feel influences the actions you show up and take on a day-to-day basis. Think. Feel. Do. It's every good therapist's mantra. Let your affirmations focus you and reinforce what you want and who you want to be. Forget about everything else that you don't. Stay mindful on a moment-to-moment basis and make sure that what you're thinking, feeling, and doing are all in line. Do it enough and it becomes a healthy habit that eventually will run on automatic. Build enough healthy habits and you create a very healthy and successful lifestyle and in that moment you'll have turned your fear of success into realized success.

One of the hardest things to do in therapy is to teach a client how to not be afraid. It's counterintuitive because fear has a function. It's an innate human emotion that we experience on a cellular level and to a certain degree it serves a very purposeful protective role in our daily lives. Loud sounds. Stray animals. Sketchy situations. Unsavory characters. Our fear is designed to help us steer clear of all of these potentially dangerous situations so that we may survive another day and continue to live our best life. That fear serves us well right up until the point where it doesn't. A key distinction in combating your fear is to understand the difference between fear and danger. If one day you find yourself in the middle of the Kalahari Desert and notice a group of lions approaching you at a rapid clip, you're in danger. If one day you find yourself riding in a taxicab in Manhattan meeting some friends for dinner and you suddenly get nervous, you're experiencing fear. Fear is defined by Merriam-Webster Dictionary as an unpleasant, often strong emotion caused by anticipation or awareness of danger. Danger is defined as exposure or liability to injury, pain, harm, or loss. Fear can be either real or imagined. Danger is only real. Fear is about perceived threats. Danger is about identified threats. Fear is an emotion. Danger is a situation. Fear is anticipatory. Danger is live action. Danger is a circumstance. Like Charlamagne says here, fear is a choice. And it's one we can control and mitigate with practice. The other, we need to avoid at all costs. A technique I've found that works wonders with clients is the idea of making fear your friend. I love Charlamagne's X-Men analogy because it's the exact same concept. You take what can be perceived as being your biggest weakness and turn it into your biggest strength. He turned his fear of failure into a work ethic that pushed him to the highest heights of his career. Don't let the fear immobilize you, instead let it motivate you! Les Brown talked extensively about "Feeling the fear and doing it anyway!" The trick is to simply notice the fear, be aware that it's present, and don't try to stop it, just push right past it with action. When we talk about having a fear of failure this technique works exceedingly well because it can push you to work harder and longer than anyone else in your field because you're deathly afraid of not achieving and you don't want to see what that life looks like. A healthy fear of failure can be your best friend because it can help you achieve high levels of success. What's key here is to allow it to push you toward success but not make you miserable in the process. Fear will only get you so far. Ultimately it's your purpose that will pull you the rest of the way home.

Another takeaway from this chapter is the very subtle but extremely important need to develop a vocabulary for what you're actually experiencing. Enter Kanye's "nervous breakdown." Having grown up black in rural South Carolina, I understand culturally exactly what that phrase means. But as a psychiatrist trying to assess symptoms in order to help a client feel better that term doesn't give me the information I need. Is it anxiety? Is it depression? Is it psychosis or some other thought disorder? Are there physical symptoms you're experiencing that we need to determine the source of? Clinically it's hard for me to help you wrap your arms around a "nervous breakdown" because that's a very nebulous thing. But if you tell me you're having palpitations, shortness of breath, and sweaty palms up to four times a day that last for five to ten minutes per episode, I can help you stop experiencing that today. Problems don't seem quite so scary when we can break them down into smaller identifiable bits and manageable pieces. Another great takeaway for us from Kanye's experience is that no one is immune to stress. Not the rich and famous and not the broke and infamous. We all have to find healthy ways to cope.

I love the way Charlamagne takes us on his journey of healing. When it comes to combating your fears the power of affirmations can be a tremendous tool in your therapeutic arsenal. Your subconscious mind will believe anything you allow in. If you can purposefully control what you feed it long enough, repeatedly enough, with enough emotional intensity, that change will take place over time. Guaranteed. We saw this when Charlamagne talked about that extended eerily unfamiliar feeling he had that he was able to identify as "peace." Again, this is why developing a proper vocabulary is important. What I noticed clinically is that feeling of peace came when Charlamagne actively engaged in a behavior that forced him to stay consistently present in the moment. Haircut. Present. Snorkeling. Present. Walking on the beach with daughters. Present. When you focus on the moment you're in, the moments that have come and gone and have yet to come don't really matter. All we have is now. Yesterday is gone so there's no need to cry over it. Tomorrow isn't here yet but you know you've faced difficult tomorrows before and come out OK so you'll be OK when this next one comes too. Breathe. Stay present in the now. What's now is what's real. Trust yourself and your ability to handle whatever comes next. Trust that you'll be OK. Take solace in the knowing. Find your peace. Better yet, sit quietly and let your peace find you.

Acknowledgments

There are only two people I want to thank for this book. First and foremost is God. Whatever you call God—be it Jehovah, Allah, Buddha, Yahweh, Elohim, Abba, El Elyon, El Roi, El Shaddai, Yahweh Yireh, Yahweh Nissi, Jehovah Rapha, or Yahweh Shalom—whatever you call the creator, lord of all the worlds, just give all praises to him and know that there is something out here bigger than all of us. Knowing God is the foundation and beginning of choosing faith over fear.

I also want to thank my therapist. This book wouldn't have been possible without you. I've noticed you have been taking a lot more vacations lately and I'm starting to think it's my fault that you need so many breaks. I know, I know I'm a lot. Thank you for making me realize there's power in being vulnerable.

Oh, and with that said, one last thing I want to acknowledge is a quote from TheKillosopher, Criss Jami:

> *To share your weakness is to make yourself vulnerable;*
> *to make yourself vulnerable is to show your strength.*

ABOUT THE AUTHOR

Charlamagne Tha God is the cohost of the nationally syndicated hip-hop iHeartRadio program *The Breakfast Club*, a featured television personality, and the *New York Times*–bestselling author of *Black Privilege*. He is also a social media influencer; an executive producer with his own production company, CThaGod World LLC; and cohost of the popular podcast *The Brilliant Idiots*. Born and raised in a small town in South Carolina, Charlamagne quickly rose to become one of today's most unique and compelling media personalities. His controversial opinions and provocative celebrity interviews help drive the daily national conversation about issues related to hip-hop, race, society, and politics. *Shook One* is his second book.